How to Use this Book

Matched to the National Curriculum, this Collins Year 4 Reading Comprehension workbook is designed to improve comprehension skills.

Diverse and engaging texts including **fiction**, **non-fiction** and **poetry**.

Tests **increase in difficulty** as you work through the book.

Questions split into three levels of difficulty – **Challenge 1**, **Challenge 2** and **Challenge 3** – to help progression.

Total marks boxes for recording progress and '**How am I doing**' checks for self-evaluation.

Starter test recaps skills covered in Year 3.

Three **Progress tests** included throughout the book for ongoing assessment and monitoring progress.

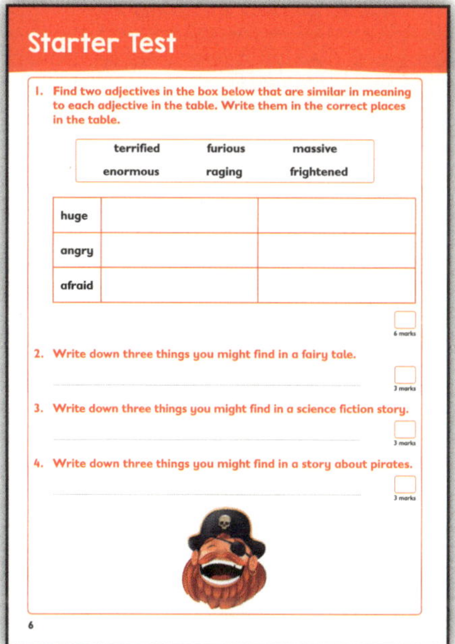

Answers are included at the back of the book.

Author: Alison Head

Contents

How to Use This Book		1
Reading Comprehension at Home		4
Starter Test		6
The Last Bear by Hannah Gold	Fiction	14
Maps of the United Kingdom: Merseyside by Rachel Dixon and Livi Gosling	Non-fiction	16
Night Flight by Laura Mucha	Poetry	18
The Day I Fell Into a Fairytale by Ben Miller	Fiction	20
Paul the Octopus by Matt Oldfield	Non-fiction	22
Follow Me by Petonelle Archer	Poetry	24
Matilda by Roald Dahl	Fiction	26
Ancient Colour From the Earth by Clive Gifford	Non-fiction	28
Flying by JM Westrup	Poetry	30
Progress Test 1		32
Tom's Midnight Garden by Philippa Pearce	Fiction	36
Young Heroes: Inspirational Children *From Around the World* by Lula Bridgeport	Non-fiction	39
The Sound Collector by Roger McGough	Poetry	42
Amina's Voice by Hena Khan	Fiction	45
Lauren Child	Non-fiction	48

Cat by Ted Hughes	Poetry	**51**
Progress Test 2		**54**
The Butterfly Lion by Michael Morpurgo	Fiction	**58**
Peru	Non-fiction	**62**
Sun and Flowers by Madison Julius Cawein	Poetry	**66**
The Beast of Buckingham Palace by David Walliams	Fiction	**70**
Wind and Water Power	Non-fiction	**74**
The Magic of the Brain by Jenny Joseph	Poetry	**78**
When Hitler Stole Pink Rabbit by Judith Kerr	Fiction	**82**
Progress Test 3		**86**
Answers		**90**

Acknowledgments

The author and publisher are grateful to the copyright holders for permission to use quoted materials and images. 'The Shell' by John Foster was taken from: I am the Seed that Grew the Tree – published by Nosy Crow Ltd; 'Charlotte's Web' by EB White, was published by Puffin Classics. © Copyright EB White, 1952; 'What a Waste: Rubbish, Recycling and Protecting Our Planet' by Jess French. Published by DK Children. © Copyright 2019; 'Night Flight' by Laura Mucha, taken from: Dear Ugly Sisters and Other Poems', published by Otter-Barry Books © Copyright Laura Mucha. Used by permission of David Higham Associates on behalf of the author; 'The Day I Fell into a Fairytale' by Ben Miller. Published by Simon & Schuster Children's UK. © Ben Miller 2020; 'Follow Me' by Petronelle Archer was taken from: A First Poetry Book, published by Macmillan's Children's Books. © Petronelle Archer. Used by permission of the author; 'Matilda' by Roald Dahl, published by Puffin Classics. © Roald Dahl; 'Flying' by JM Westrup, taken from: I am the Seed that Grew the Planet. Published by Nosy Crow Ltd; 'Fangs' by Malorie Blackman, published by Tamarind. © Malorie Blackman 2015; 'Stories for Boys Who Dare to be Different' by Ben Brooks, published by Quercus (Hachette) © Copyright Ben Brooks. Reproduced by permission of Quercus Children's Books, an imprint of Hachette Children's Books, Carmelite House, 50 Victoria Embankment, London EC4Y 0DZ; 'Young Heroes: Inspirational Children From Around the World" by Lula Bridgeport, Published by Stripes Publishing © Lula Bridgeport; 'Amina's Voice' by Hena Khan, published by Salaam Reads / Simon & Schuster Books for Young Readers. © Hena Khan 2018; 'So Where Do You Get Your Ideas From?' by Lauren Child, taken from: Flights of Fancy: Stories, Pictures and Inspiration from Ten Children's Laureates, published by Walker Books. © Lauren Child; 'The Star Outside my Window' by Onjali Rauf, published by Orion Books. © Onjali Rauf. Reproduced by permission of Orion Children's Books, an imprint of Hachette Children's Books, Carmelite House, 50 Victoria Embankment, London EC4Y 0DZ; 'Peru' taken from The Travel Book: A Journey Through Every Country in the World., published By Lonely Planet Kids; Sun and Flowers by Madison Julius Cawein; 'Wind and Water Power' was taken from Science Encyclopedia: Atom Smashing, Food Chemistry, Animals, Space and More! Published by National Geographic Kids; 'The Sun and Planets' taken from The Universe as You've Never Seen It Before: Knowledge Encyclopaedia Space! Published by DK;

'Look at all Those Monkeys' was taken from: 'A Children's Treasury of Milligan, by Spike Milligan. Published by Virgin Books. © Spike Milligan, 2006; The Boy Who Grew Dragons (Piccadilly Press, 2018) by Andy Shepherd. Text copyright © Andy Shepherd, 2018. First published in the UK by Bonnier Books UK Ltd; The Magic of the Brain by Jenny Joseph. Reproduced by permission of Johnson & Alcock Ltd; Tom's Midnight Garden by Philippa Pearce. Reproduced with permission of the Licensor through PLSclear; Cat from Collected Poems for Children by Ted Hughes. Reproduced by permission of Faber and Faber Ltd; The Last Bear by Hannah Gold. Reprinted by permission of HarperCollins Publishers Ltd © 2021 Hannah Gold; The Butterfly Lion by Michael Morpurgo. Reprinted by permission of HarperCollins Publishers Ltd © 1996 Michael Morpurgo; Women In Science: 50 Fearless Pioneers Who Changed the World by Rachel Ignotofsky reproduced by permission of Hodder Children's Books, an imprint of Hachette Children's Books, Carmelite House, 50 Victoria Embankment, London, EC4Y 0DZ; Paul the Octopus from Unbelievable Football: The Most Incredible True Football Stories by Matt Oldfield reproduced by permission of Hodder Children's Books, an imprint of Hachette Children's Books, Carmelite House, 50 Victoria Embankment, London, EC4Y 0DZ; British Museum: So You Think You Got it Bad? A Kid's Life in Ancient Egypt by Chae Strathie. Text Copyright © Nosy Crow Limited 2020. Reproduced with permission of Nosy Crow Ltd; When Hitler Stole Pink Rabbit by Judith Kerr. Reprinted by permission of HarperCollins Publishers Ltd © 2008 Judith Kerr; The Beast of Buckingham Palace by David Walliams. Reprinted by permission of HarperCollins Publishers Ltd © 2021 David Walliams; "The Sound Collector" by Roger McGough from "Pillow Talk" (© Roger McGough, 1990) is printed by permission of United Agents (www.unitedagents.co.uk) on behalf of Roger McGough; The Colours of History: How Colours Shaped the World, written by Clive Gifford and illustrated by Marc-Etienne Peintre, published by QED Publishing, an imprint of The Quarto Group, copyright ©2018. Reproduced by permission of Quarto Publishing Plc. Maps of the United Kingdom, written by Rachel Dixon and illustrated by Livi Gosling, published by Wide-Eyed Editions, an imprint of The Quarto Group, copyright © 2018. Reproduced by permission of Quarto Publishing Plc.

All Illustrations and images are ©Shutterstock.com and ©HarperCollinsPublishers Ltd.

Published by Collins
An imprint of HarperCollinsPublishers
1 London Bridge Street
London SE1 9GF

HarperCollinsPublishers
Macken House, 39/40 Mayor Street Upper,
Dublin 1, D01 C9W8, Ireland

© HarperCollinsPublishers Limited 2025

ISBN 978-0-00-846758-6

First published 2021; this edition published 2025

10 9 8 7 6

All rights reserved. No part of this publication may be reproduced, stored in a retrieval system, or transmitted, in any form or by any means, electronic, mechanical, photocopying, recording or otherwise, without the prior permission of Collins.

Without limiting the exclusive rights of any author, contributor or the publisher of this publication, any unauthorised use of this publication to train generative artificial intelligence (AI) technologies is expressly prohibited. HarperCollins also exercise their rights under Article 4(3) of the Digital Single Market Directive 2019/790 and expressly reserve this publication from the text and data mining exception.

British Library Cataloguing in Publication Data.

A CIP record of this book is available from the British Library.

Publisher: Fiona McGlade
Author: Alison Head
Editorial: Shelley Teasdale and Fiona Watson
Cover Design: Sarah Duxbury
Inside Concept Design and Page Layout: Ian Wrigley
Printed in the United Kingdom

Reading Comprehension at Home

These activities can be easily carried out at home when reading for pleasure with your child, or when your child is reading for pleasure on their own. They will help build your child's comprehension skills and are fun to do.

Vocabulary building

Make good use of journey times to play word games that help to build up your child's vocabulary. Give them a topic and ask them to think of a word related to that topic beginning with each letter of the alphabet. Alternatively, start with an adjective and ask them to see how many more they can think of with a similar meaning. Introduce new words one at a time and revisit them often, so your child gets used to using them in sentences.

Judge a book by its cover

When you are choosing a book with your child at the library or bookshop, ask them to predict what might happen in the story based on the picture and the words on the cover. Show them the 'blurb' on the back and explain that it is there to give readers a taste of what is inside. Ask them to explain why they do, or do not, want to read that book.

Lead by example

It's good for your child to see the adults around them reading for pleasure. Discuss with them the books you loved reading when you were their age, and offer to read them one of your favourites.

What's inside?

Show your child the different ways the information in non-fiction books is organised to help readers find their way around the book. You could even set up a treasure hunt in a selection of non-fiction books, where your child has to solve the clues and use the contents pages and indexes to find specific pieces of information.

Not just books!

If your child is a digital native, harness their love of the screen (sparingly) to spark an interest in reading. Search out well-written, child-friendly websites about topics they love and spend some time exploring them together. Look for fun facts and interesting vocabulary, and explore how information on the web is organised to help people find what they want.

Make connections

When you are reading with your child, encourage them to make connections between the book and their own experiences. For example, you may want to ask them if they remember a time when they had a similar experience to a character in the book; if they can think of other poems with similar characters, settings or themes; or if they've seen or heard about the information you read in a non-fiction book.

Join the library

Borrowing books from your local library is an easy and inexpensive way to ensure that your child experiences a wide range of books. Children's librarians are experts at ensuring their collections are full of well-loved classics, new releases, comics, audio stories and interesting non-fiction. Many local libraries also run story sessions and arrange activity sessions aimed at encouraging reading.

Words in focus

Give your child time to work on words they find difficult to read. Don't be too quick to read it for them, but show them strategies they could use, for example breaking it down into syllables. Make sure your child understands the meaning of the word before moving on.

Starter Test

1. **Find two adjectives in the box below that are similar in meaning to each adjective in the table. Write them in the correct places in the table.**

| terrified | furious | massive |
| enormous | raging | frightened |

huge		
angry		
afraid		

6 marks

2. **Write down three things you might find in a fairy tale.**

3 marks

3. **Write down three things you might find in a science fiction story.**

3 marks

4. **Write down three things you might find in a story about pirates.**

3 marks

5. 'A hideous beast stood before me.'
    Circle a word below that describes the beast.

    beautiful   ugly

6. 'We heard a piercing shriek.'
    Circle a word below that tells you what they heard.

    a scream   a song

7. 'Suddenly, the strange light vanished.'
    Circle a word below that describes what happened to
    the light.

    it faded   it disappeared

8. 'Harvest mice are tiny, agile creatures.'
    Circle a word below that describes harvest mice.

    nimble   rare

9. 'The flames spread swiftly through the crowded streets.'
    Circle a word below that describes how the flames spread.

    chaotically   rapidly

10. Explain what 'fiction' means.

....

1 mark

11. Give an example of a type of non-fiction writing.

....

1 mark

12. What type of book do you think *The Adventures of Billy the Talking Mouse* might be? Circle your answer.

fiction   **non-fiction**

1 mark

13. What type of book do you think *Volcanoes* might be? Circle your answer.

fiction   **non-fiction**

1 mark

14. Draw lines to match each feature of a non-fiction book with the job that it does.

Contents page   Alphabetical list of topics with their page numbers, found at the back of the book.

Index   Numbers on each page, to help you find the right page.

Glossary   List of chapters or sections with their page numbers, found at the front of the book.

Page numbers   Alphabetical list of words and their meanings, usually found at the back of the book.

4 marks

***The Boy Who Grew Dragons* by Andy Shepherd**

It started about a year ago. And it was all Grandad's fault. Well, his and the jam tart's. I was just licking the last of it off my fingers when he said:

'We should grow our own, Chipstick.'

'Jam tarts?' I asked.

'Raspberries.' He grinned. 'Then we could make our own jam for Nana's tarts. We could mix them up too. Strawberry and blackberry, gooseberry and raspberry – just think of the possibilities. *Deeeelicious!*'

It did make a pretty good picture in my head, a vast plate-sized jam tart with different-coloured sections like a multi-topping pizza.

15. What type of book do you think this extract is from? Circle your answer.

fiction　　　　　　　　　　**non-fiction**

1 mark

16. Give a reason for your answer.

....

2 marks

17. Write down three fruits mentioned in the text.

....

1 mark

18. Do you think Grandad likes Nana's tarts? Give a reason for your answer.

....

1 mark

19. What type of food does the narrator compare the tart he imagines with?

....

1 mark

***So You Think You've Got It Bad? A Kid's Life in Ancient Egypt* by Chae Strathie**

In ancient Egypt, pretty much ALL of the houses were made of mud. OK, it wasn't the gloopy kind. No, these houses were made from mud bricks that had been hardened in the sun.

Sometimes extremely wealthy people lined the outside of their homes with white limestone, which was SUPER-PRICEY but made the houses GLITTER in the sunshine.

SOUNDS SWANKY, but imagine your mum's face if you leaned against the shiny white wall with dirty hands. She'd have you down at the Nile fetching water to clean it faster than you could say "JUMPING JACKALS!"

20. What type of book do you think this extract is from? Circle your answer.

    fiction　　　　　　　　**non-fiction**

1 mark

21. Give a reason for your answer.

1 mark

22. Write another word similar in meaning to 'gloopy'.

1 mark

23. Write another word similar in meaning to 'wealthy'.

1 mark

24. Why do you think the writer has used capital letters for some words and phrases?

1 mark

The Shell **by John Foster**

On the shelf in my bedroom stands a shell.
If I hold it close, I can smell
The salty sea.
I can hear the slap
Of the waves as they lap
The sandy shore.
I can feel once more
The tickling tide
As it gently flows between my toes.

25. Do poems always rhyme? ....

I mark

26. Find and copy a word that rhymes with each word in the table.

shell	
slap	
shore	
flows	

I mark

27. Find and copy an example of how the poet has used the senses to describe the sea.

....

I mark

28. According to the poem, how does the sea smell?

....

I mark

29. Do you think the narrator likes the seaside? Give a reason for your answer.

....

I mark

Charlotte's Web by EB White

The night seemed long. Wilbur's stomach was empty and his mind was full. And when your stomach is empty and your mind is full, it's always hard to sleep.

A dozen times during the night Wilbur woke and stared into blackness, listening to the sounds and trying to figure out what time it was. A barn is never perfectly quiet. Even at midnight there is usually something stirring.

The first time he woke, he heard Templeton gnawing a hole in the grain bin. Templeton's teeth scraped loudly against the wood and made quite a racket. "That crazy rat!" thought Wilbur.

30. Using information from the text, tick one box in each row to show whether each statement is true or false.

		True	False
a)	Wilbur is hungry.		
b)	The barn was silent.		
c)	Templeton is a rat.		

3 marks

31. '…his mind was full.' What do you think this means?

....

1 mark

32. 'A dozen times…' How many is a 'dozen'?

....

1 mark

33. Find and copy the word that tells you it was dark in the barn.

....

1 mark

34. Find and copy two pieces of evidence that tell you that Templeton's chewing was noisy.

....

2 marks

What a Waste: Rubbish, Recycling and Protecting Our Planet by Jess French

Imagine if we ran out of clean water to use. We need to drink it to survive. Water isn't just for drinking, though. It is used to make products and for lots of other things. Water is cleaned for reuse, but this process needs electricity. Saving water helps to make sure we all have enough!

Up to 6 litres (1.3 gallons) of water is used with one flush. In toilets with big and small flush buttons, the small button uses less water.

Up to 12 litres (2.6 gallons) of water pour out of a running tap a minute. Turn taps off when you're not using them during teeth brushing and face washing.

35. What is needed to clean water? ....

1 mark

36. According to the text, how can we make sure we all have enough water?

1 mark

37. What is 1.3 gallons in litres?

1 mark

38. Why are toilets with big and small flush buttons a good idea?

1 mark

39. How long does it take for 12 litres of water to pour out of a running tap?

1 mark

40. How can you save water when brushing your teeth?

1 mark

Total: _______/58 marks

The Last Bear

You had to really inhale deeply. She didn't have his nose, but after weeks of practising she had finally managed to smell the hard ice of the glaciers in the North Pole. They smelled sharp and clean, like glass bottles. He also showed her how to tell which way the wind was blowing and if there was snow coming, or a storm due, or even rain in the air.

Best of all on this particular afternoon, he taught her to listen. Not just listen like you and me listen. But *really* listen. When she cocked her head and opened her ears, she could hear snowflakes settle on the mountaintops, the creaks and groans of cargo ships out of sight and even Dad's sighs on the breeze. Then, when the sleet had cleared and the sun reappeared and they couldn't tell if it was afternoon, evening or even the next day, he taught her how to listen to the island itself.

Of course, at first she had no idea what he was doing. She'd watched curiously as he lay flat on the ground with his ear pressed to the earth. Long seconds passed and the only sound was the gentle exhalation of her own breath.

'What are you listening to?' she asked at last.

With no answer forthcoming, the only thing to do was to find out for herself.

She copied the way Bear had flattened himself on the ground and lay with her own ear pressed to the earth.

By Hannah Gold

Challenge 1

1 What does 'inhale' mean? .... ☐ 1 mark

2 What familiar object does the narrator say glaciers smell like?

.... ☐ 1 mark

3 What are glaciers made of? .... ☐ 1 mark

4 What type of ships are referred to? .... ☐ 1 mark

1 'She didn't have his nose…' Explain what this phrase means.

1 mark

2 'But *really* listen.' Why do you think the writer has used italics for the word 'really'?

1 mark

3 Where do you think the story is set? Find and copy two pieces of evidence from the text to support your answer.

3 marks

Challenge 3

1 How long had the girl been learning from Bear? Give a reason from the text to support your answer.

2 marks

2 What sounds can the girl hear after Bear has taught her to '*really* listen'?

3 marks

3 Do you think the girl is surprised when Bear does not answer her question? Give a reason for your answer.

1 mark

Total: _______ / 15 marks

😐 **Had a go** ☐ 🙂 **Getting there** ☐ 😃 **Got it!** ☐

Maps of the United Kingdom: Merseyside

Liverpool, the biggest city in Merseyside, is perhaps most famous as the birthplace of the Beatles, but the Fab Four aren't the only chart-topping things about Merseyside: this is one of the country's sporting hubs, home to the Grand National at Aintree and two world-famous Premiership football teams, Liverpool FC and Everton. In-between fixtures, why not make a magical mystery tour of the city or take a trip on the Mersey Ferry? From the water, you can spot two birds perched atop the Liver Building – one looks across the docks and out to sea, making sure sailors make it safely back to port, while the other watches over the city, keeping its citizens safe. And once you've worked up an appetite, why not try some scouse? This stew has given Scousers their nickname – and a city of full bellies.

WILLIAM GLADSTONE   1809–1898

The Liberal politician from Liverpool was the prime minister four times (more than anyone else) and chancellor four times.

WAYNE ROONEY   B. 1985

The footballer from Croxteth began his career at Everton and is the all-time record goalscorer for Manchester United and England.

LITA ROZA   1926–2008

The singer from Liverpool was the first woman to have a No. 1 hit record in the UK, with (*How Much Is*) *That Doggie in the Window?* in 1953.

MIKE MYERS   B. 1963

The Canadian-born actor's parents were from Liverpool – he is the voice of Shrek and the star of *Wayne's World* and *Austin Powers*.

CILLA BLACK   1943–2015

Born Priscilla White, the singer and entertainer rose to fame during the "Swinging Sixties" alongside her friends the Beatles. She later became a popular television presenter.

By Rachel Dixon and Livi Gosling

1 Where is the Grand National held? ....

1 mark

2 What is a 'ferry'? ....

1 mark

3 When was Wayne Rooney born? ....

1 mark

4 According to the text, what is 'scouse'? ....

1 mark

Challenge 2

1 What is another name for The Beatles? ....

1 mark

2 What does the phrase 'magical mystery tour' suggest about what
   a visit to Liverpool might be like?

....

1 mark

Challenge 3

1 What evidence is there to suggest that The Beatles are very famous?

....

1 mark

2 Why do the birds on the Liver Building face in different directions?

....

1 mark

3 Find two pieces of evidence that support the idea that the dish scouse
   is popular.

....

....

2 marks

Total: _______ / 10 marks

😐 **Had a go** ☐   🙂 **Getting there** ☐   😃 **Got it!** ☐

Night Flight

Tonight I fancy a flight,
so I shuffle my short feathers
and jump.

Clusters of city lights
stretch, spread and sprawl
into sparkling starfish.

A whisper of clouds
tickles my feet.
A current lifts me like a leaf —

I float, I glide,
I hold my feathered wings out wide
and watch the world beneath.

The occasional plane passes
The odd meteorite. Together
we set the sky alight.

Flight is always best at night.

By Laura Mucha

Challenge 1

1 '…I shuffle my short feathers…' Circle the word below that is closest in meaning to the word 'shuffle' as it is used in this line.

scuffle　　　　**sort**　　　　**rearrange**　　　　**shorten**

1 mark

2 Find something natural and something man-made that joins the bird to light up the sky.

Natural	a)
Man-made	b)

2 marks

3 Find and copy two words at the end of lines that rhyme.

____

1 mark

1 What does the line 'stretch, spread and sprawl' suggest about the size of the city?

____

1 mark

2 'I float, I glide…' Give two ways that this line supports the idea that the bird's flight is effortless.

____

____

2 marks

3 How does the phrase 'A current lifts me like a leaf –' support the idea that the breeze easily lifts the bird?

____

____

1 mark

Challenge 3

1 The poet uses alliteration in the line 'stretch, spread and sprawl'. What other two words in this part of the poem continue this alliteration?

____

2 marks

2 What do you think the line 'A whisper of clouds' means?

____

1 mark

3 Why do you think the bird prefers flying at night? Support your answer with two pieces of evidence from the text.

____

____

2 marks

Total: _______ / 13 marks

😐 **Had a go** ☐   🙂 **Getting there** ☐   😃 **Got it!** ☐

The Day I Fell Into a Fairytale

Lightning crackled in the sky, and thunder rolled out across the valley. The mound of earth began to shake and its peak trembled and quivered, until suddenly a gleaming white enamel flagpole popped out of the top!

Up and up climbed the flagpole, rising out of the ground like a beanstalk in a fairytale.

Once it had reached its full height, it paused before it too began to quiver and shake. Because the flagpole was just the beginning.

Cracks crazed their way across the common, as the turf began to warp and split, and something truly enormous began to emerge.

A roof. A colossal, aluminium roof! Up and up it buckled, pushed by the cinder block walls emerging from the ground beneath it. Earth tumbled away and, like a giant rising from its slumber, an entire building began to rise. Girders popped into place, door frames righted themselves, and sheets of plate glass found their groove. Once everything was in place, the entire structure fell silent.

Still the rain lashed down, washing everything clean.

Then the heavy grey clouds cleared, and a full moon shone bright as a penny. The wind calmed and the rain stopped.

In a nearby field, a cock crowed. It was morning now, and across the valley the pale dawn sky brightened to blue. Soon, the first rays of sunlight were chasing across the still-sleeping village. And there, at the bottom of the hill, smack dab in the middle of the common, what had started as a mound of earth no bigger than a molehill, was now a brand-new supermarket.

By Ben Miller

Challenge 1

1. '…a gleaming white enamel flagpole…' Write another word with a similar meaning to 'gleaming'. ___________________

1 mark

2. '…the turf began to warp…' Circle the word below which is closest in meaning to 'warp'.

> **twitch** **slide** **distort** **grow**

1 mark

3 '...something truly enormous began to emerge.' Write another word

with a similar meaning to 'emerge'.

1 mark

4 What is the roof of the structure made from?

1 mark

Challenge 2

1 What does the phrase 'lashed down' suggest about the rain?

1 mark

2 Find two words from different parts of the text that describe the

size of the structure.

2 marks

3 a) Find the simile the narrator uses to describe the moon.

1 mark

b) Why do you think this is a good choice of simile?

1 mark

Challenge 3

1 '...rising out of the ground like a beanstalk in a fairytale.' Find a reference
to something else in the text that you might expect to find in a fairytale.

1 mark

2 What might the villagers think when they wake up and see
the supermarket?

1 mark

3 What do you think might happen next in the story?

1 mark

Total: _______ / 12 marks

😐 **Had a go** ☐   🙂 **Getting there** ☐   😃 **Got it!** ☐

Paul the Octopus

'What a clever animal!' People say that all the time. You hear it whenever their dogs/cats/lizards learn to sit/roll/bake cakes (OK, maybe not that last one), but if you want to hear about a properly clever creature, let me introduce you to Paul the Octopus.

Paul was born in a Sea Life Centre in the pretty British seaside town of Weymouth in 2008, but as a hatchling (that's what they call a baby octopus, by the way) he moved abroad to another Sea Life Centre in Oberhausen, Germany. It was there that people started to notice Paul's special talents.

The first sign that he was a really clever octopus was his ability to open jars and boxes as easily as a human being. That was a cool trick, but what else could Paul do, they wondered? Predict football results, perhaps?

The Sea Life Centre workers came up with a game to test him during Euro 2008. Before each match that the Germany national team played at the tournament, they placed two clear plastic boxes in front of Paul. Each box had food inside – either a mussel or an oyster – and a national flag on the front. Apparently, whichever box Paul opened first was the team that he thought would win the match!

'What about draws?' you ask. Well, sorry, that wasn't an option. But never mind, no one likes draws anyway…

Paul's record at Euro 2008 was pretty good – four correct predictions out of six.

Unbelievable Football: The Most Incredible True Football Stories (You Never Knew)
by Matt Oldfield

Challenge 1

1   What does the word 'hatchling' mean, as it is used in this text?

I mark

2   'Predict football results, perhaps?' Circle the word below that is closest in meaning to 'predict'.

invent   **create**   **forget**   **foretell**

I mark

3 Find a word in the text with a similar meaning to 'animal'.

I mark

4 Write another word that is similar in meaning to 'tournament'.

I mark

Challenge 2

1 Find an example of something an octopus eats.

I mark

2 What evidence is there in the text to support the idea that not every octopus can open jars and boxes?

I mark

3 What national flag would always have been on one of the plastic boxes Paul had to choose between?

I mark

Challenge 3

1 In football, a draw is where both teams score the same number of goals. Why could Paul not predict draws?

I mark

2 Why do you think the writer says that nobody likes draws?

I mark

3 Do you think that Paul's record – four correct predictions out of six – means he could really predict the result of football matches? Give a reason for your answer.

I mark

Total: _______ / 10 marks

😐 **Had a go** ☐   🙂 **Getting there** ☐   😃 **Got it!** ☐

23

Follow Me

Follow me, follow me
Under the alder tree
Down to the bank where the sleek
otters play,
Emperor dragonfly
Kingfisher flashing by
Blue, green and gold of a midsummer
    day.

Follow me, follow me
By the bare alder tree
Bittersweet berries splash red on the snow,
Mirror carp, pike and bream
Held in an icy dream
Watching pale shadows from darkness
    below.

By Petonelle Archer

Challenge 1

1 Circle the word below that is closest in meaning to 'sleek'.

   slick　　　　**elegant**　　　　**glossy**　　　　**black**

   1 mark

2 What does the word 'midsummer' mean?

   ____

   1 mark

3 'Watching pale shadows…' Find a word from the second half of the
   poem that contrasts with 'pale'. _______________________________

   1 mark

4 Which word in the second half of the poem tells you it is cold?

....

1 mark

Challenge 2

1 How do you know that the 'bank' the poet is writing about is a riverbank?

....

1 mark

2 What two animals contribute to the 'Blue, green and gold of a midsummer day'?

....

2 marks

3 What does the phrase 'flashing by' suggest about the kingfisher?

....

1 mark

Challenge 3

1 Why is the alder tree 'bare' in the second half of the poem?

....

1 mark

2 'Held in an icy dream…' What does this line suggest about the fish ('carp, pike and bream') and the river?

....

....

2 marks

3 What do the people above look like to the fish looking up from the water?

....

1 mark

Total: _______ / 12 marks

☺ **Had a go** ☐   ☺ **Getting there** ☐   ☺ **Got it!** ☐

Matilda

It's a funny thing about mothers and fathers. Even when their own child is the most disgusting little blister you could ever imagine, they still think that he or she is wonderful.

Some parents go further. They become so blinded by adoration they manage to convince themselves their child has qualities of genius.

Well, there is nothing very wrong with all this. It's the way of the world. It's only when the parents begin telling *us* about the brilliance of their own revolting offspring, that we start shouting, 'Bring us a basin! We're going to be sick!'

School teachers suffer a good deal from having to listen to this sort of twaddle from proud parents, but they usually get their own back when the time comes to write the end-of-term reports. If I were a teacher I would cook up some real scorchers for the children of doting parents. 'Your son Maximilian,' I would write, 'is a total wash-out. I hope you have a family business you can push him into when he leaves school because he sure as heck won't get a job anywhere else.' Or if I were feeling lyrical that day, I might write, 'It's a curious truth that grasshoppers have their hearing-organs in the sides of the abdomen. Your daughter Vanessa, judging by what she's learnt this term, has no hearing-organs at all.'

I might even delve deeper into natural history and say, 'The periodical cicada spends six years as a grub underground, and no more than six *days* as a free creature of sunlight and air. Your son Wilfred has spent six years as a grub in this school and we are still waiting for him to emerge from the chrysalis.'

By Roald Dahl

Challenge I

1 What does 'offspring' mean? ....

I mark

2 '…this sort of twaddle…' Write another word with a similar meaning

to 'twaddle'. ....

I mark

3 The writer uses the adjective 'disgusting' to describe some children.
Find another adjective in the text with a similar meaning.

1 mark

Challenge 2

1 Why do you think the narrator refers to the child as a 'blister' at the start of the text?

1 mark

2 What is the narrator referring to when he writes about the child's

'hearing-organs'?

1 mark

Challenge 3

1 Parents and teachers don't always see children the same way. According to the text, how do parents see their children and how do teachers see the children they teach?

a) Parents

b) Teachers

2 marks

2 Which phrase shows that the writer thinks it is natural for parents to think their children are special?

1 mark

3 How do you think a parent might feel if their child's school report contained the kind of comments the writer has written? Include two ideas in your answer.

2 marks

Total: _______ / 10 marks

 **Had a go**    **Getting there**   **Got it!**

Ancient Colour From the Earth

Yellow ochre

In 1940, four teenagers were exploring the woods near their home town of Montignac, France, when one of them made an astonishing discovery. A deep hole led the boys into the previously unknown Lascaux Cave. Its walls were covered in colourful prehistoric cave art, much of it painted in yellow ochre.

Clay colour

Yellow ochre is an earthy pigment made from clay containing iron oxide. This clay is found in many places in the world, and early people ground it down into a powder. Mixing the powder with plant sap or water made paint that could be dabbed onto rock using hands, leaves, tree bark or thin animal bones. At Lascaux, some of the artwork was spray-painted onto the rock walls by blowing paint through a reed or hollow bone.

Made to last

The paintings discovered by the teenagers featured yellows and reds made from ochre. There was also black, which came from charcoal. The paintings depicted more than 2,000 different figures, mostly animals such as horses, bulls and stags – and even a rhinoceros! Unlike some other pigments, yellow ochre does not decay or fade quickly, especially when it is not exposed to sunlight. Many of Lascaux's cave paintings are thought to be more than 17,000 years old.

Around the world

Royal tombs in ancient Egypt were often decorated with yellow ochre walls, and Australian Aboriginals painted with it, too. It was later used by many famous artists including Rembrandt, Renoir and Raphael. By the 18th century, France had become a centre for the production of yellow ochre. The Huli tribe in Papua New Guinea and the Fulani people in western Africa still work with yellow ochre, using it as make-up for ceremonies, covering their entire face in the colour.

The Colours of History: How Colours Shaped the World by Clive Gifford

Challenge 1

1 Write another word with a similar meaning to 'astonishing'.

1 mark

2 '...hollow bone...' What does 'hollow' mean?

1 mark

3 '...earthy pigment...' Circle the word below that is closest in meaning to 'pigment'.

    colour   **brush**   **cave**   **clay**

1 mark

Challenge 2

1 'This clay is found in many places in the world...' Which section of the text gives more information about this?

1 mark

2 '...even a rhinoceros!' Why do you think the writer put an exclamation mark at the end of this sentence?

1 mark

3 Give one way plants may have been used in the making of cave art.

1 mark

Challenge 3

1 Do you think the teenagers were looking for the cave when they went exploring in the woods? Give a reason for your answer.

1 mark

2 Look at the section 'Made to last'. Can you suggest two reasons why the Lascaux cave paintings were still 'colourful', even after 17,000 years?

2 marks

Total: _______ / 9 marks

😐 **Had a go** ☐   🙂 **Getting there** ☐   😄 **Got it!** ☐

Flying

I saw the moon,
One windy night,
Flying so fast –
All silvery white –
Over the sky
Like a toy balloon
Loose from its string –
A runaway moon.
The frosty stars
Went racing past,
Chasing her on
Ever so fast.
Then everyone said,
"It's the clouds that fly,
And the stars and moon
Stand still in the sky."
But I don't mind –
I saw the moon
Sailing away
Like a toy
Balloon.

By JM Westrup

Challenge 1

1. 'Flying so fast –' Find and copy two other words or phrases that show how fast the moon appears to be moving.

____

I mark

2. Find something else that is said to fly in the poem.

____

I mark

3. What does the narrator think the moon looks like?

____

I mark

4. Does the narrator imagine the moon to be male or female? Copy the word that tells you this.

____

I mark

1 Why do you think the poet has used the phrase 'silvery white' to describe the colour of the moon?

1 mark

2 Find two references to weather given in the poem.

2 marks

3 Can you suggest why the poet uses the adjective 'frosty' to describe the stars?

1 mark

Challenge 3

1 Why does the poet compare the moon to a balloon that is 'Loose from its string'?

1 mark

2 Does what 'everyone' says change the narrator's mind about what they think they saw? Give a reason for your answer.

1 mark

3 Do you think that the narrator will look up at the night sky again the next time there is a clear night? Give a reason for your answer, based on the text.

2 marks

Total: _______ / 12 marks

 **Had a go**    **Getting there**   **Got it!**

Fangs **by Malorie Blackman**

Tap! Tap! Tap! I didn't bother to turn round. *Tap! Tap! Tap!* There it was again. Someone was tapping on the shop window and whoever it was, they obviously weren't going to go away until they had my full attention. With a sigh, I turned round.

It was a boy. A boy who blinked a lot.

He wore round glasses and he had the most serious face I'd ever seen. The boy looked at me. I looked at him. He tapped again very gently on the shop window with his fingernail and smiled – a genuine, friendly, admiring smile. And that's when I knew! This boy was all right! I beamed back at him, giving him my biggest, cheesiest, fangiest grin.

Come into the shop, I thought. *Please* come in and buy me.

I didn't want to build up my hopes. Lots of people – men and women, boys and girls – had tapped on the window and waved. Some even smiled. But none of them ever came into the shop to buy me. Mind you, a lot more people had banged on the window and looked at me with horror or disgust. But all those people who didn't like the way I looked obviously needed glasses. And if they already wore glasses, then they obviously needed *stronger* glasses. I am without a doubt the most gorgeous spider I know!

1. **What makes the narrator think that the boy tapping on the window will not give up and go away?**

____

1 mark

2. **What is the first thing the spider notices about the boy?**

____

1 mark

3. **Why do you think the boy tapped 'very gently' on the window once he had the spider's attention?**

____

1 mark

4. '...a genuine, friendly, admiring smile.' Circle the word below that is closest in meaning to 'genuine'.

cheerful   wide   sincere   silly

1 mark

5. What does the spider do to encourage the boy to come into the shop?

____

1 mark

6. '*Please* come in and buy me.' Why do you think the writer uses italics for the word 'Please'?

____

1 mark

7. Find a phrase that shows what some of the people who bang on the window feel when they look at the spider.

____

1 mark

8. Find a piece of evidence in the text to support the idea that the boy agrees that the spider is 'gorgeous'.

____

1 mark

9. Why does the spider 'sigh' when it turns round?

____

1 mark

10. What explanation does the spider give for why some people don't like how it looks?

____

1 mark

Salvador Dali

(1904–1989)

At school, Salvador would always get angry or act strangely, and the other kids would make his life miserable. He looked and acted too different to be understood.

Things didn't get much better when he moved to art school either. There, Salvador spent most of his time daydreaming. Eventually, he was expelled for causing chaos.

Salvador travelled to Paris instead, to hone his craft among other artists. He made films, sculptures, and bizarre, dreamlike paintings, where clocks melted and elephants wandered through clouds on legs as tall as skyscrapers.

Everyone loved them. Just like Salvador, they were unlike anything anyone had seen before. The strange things he used to be bullied for ended up being the things that everyone celebrated in him. Now people were excited when Salvador acted strangely.

Once, he filled his car with hundreds of cauliflowers and drove through the streets of Paris, handing them out.

Another time, he gave a lecture in a deep-sea diving suit. As a pet, he kept an ocelot, which is a large cat, like a puma, but with stripes. Whenever he took it into restaurants, the other diners would always be terrified. He'd tell them not to panic, and that it was just a normal cat that he had 'painted over'.

Salvador was so popular that all kinds of people, places and companies wanted his work. If you've ever had a Chupa Chups lollipop, then you've seen a piece of his art, because it was Salvador who designed the logo.

Ultimately, Salvador became one of the most iconic and best-loved figures in art history, all because he stayed true to himself.

11. **Why did the children at Salvador's school not understand him?**

____

1 mark

12. **Why did Salvador leave art school?**

____

1 mark

13. **'…hone his craft…' Circle the word below that is closest in meaning to 'hone'.**

forget   **develop**   **hide**   **sell**

1 mark

14. **Why do you think people liked Dali's paintings so much?**

____

1 mark

15. **What is surprising about Dali keeping an ocelot as a pet?**

____

1 mark

16. **Circle the word below that is closest in meaning to 'iconic'.**

old   **forgotten**   **famous**   **common**

1 mark

17. **The text says Salvador 'stayed true to himself.' What does this phrase mean?**

____

1 mark

18. **Are you surprised that an artist like Dali designed the Chupa Chups logo? Explain your answer.**

____

1 mark

Total: _______ / 18 marks

Tom's Midnight Garden

Slow silence, and then the grandfather clock struck for twelve. By midnight his uncle and aunt were always in bed, and asleep too, usually. Only Tom lay still open-eyed and sullen, imprisoned in wakefulness.

And at last – One! The clock struck the present hour; but, as if to show its independence of mind, went on striking – Two! For once Tom was not amused by its striking the wrong hour: Three! Four! "It's one o'clock," Tom whispered angrily over the edge of the bedclothes. "Why don't you strike one o'clock, then, as the clocks would do at home?" Instead: Five! Six! Even in his irritation, Tom could not stop counting; it had become a habit with him at night. Seven! Eight! After all, the clock was the only thing that would speak to him at all in these hours of darkness. Nine! Ten! "You are going it," thought Tom, but yawning in the midst of his unwilling admiration. Yes, and it hadn't finished yet: Eleven! Twelve! "Fancy striking midnight twice in one night!" jeered Tom, sleepily. Thirteen! proclaimed the clock, and then stopped striking.

Thirteen? Tom's mind gave a jerk: had it really struck thirteen? Even mad old clocks never struck that. He must have imagined it. Had he not been falling asleep, or already sleeping? But no, awake or dozing, he had counted up to thirteen. He was sure of it.

He was uneasy in the knowledge that this happening made some difference to him: he could feel that in his bones. The stillness had become an expectant one; the house seemed to hold its breath; the darkness pressed up to him, pressing him with a question: Come on, Tom, the clock has struck thirteen – what are you going to do about it?

By Philippa Pearce

1 What time is it at the start of the extract?

....

1 mark

2 '…open-eyed and sullen…' Write another word similar in meaning to 'sullen'.

....

1 mark

3 'Thirteen! proclaimed the clock…' Circle the word below that is closest in meaning to 'proclaimed'.

rang   **suggested**   **waited**   **announced**

1 mark

4 '…jeered Tom, sleepily.' Circle the word below that is closest in meaning to 'jeered'.

joked   **mocked**   **snapped**   **yawned**

1 mark

Challenge 2

1 'Slow silence…' How does this phrase support the idea that time felt like it was passing slowly while Tom tried to get to sleep?

....

1 mark

2 What do you think the phrase 'imprisoned in wakefulness' means?

....

....

2 marks

3 '…Tom whispered angrily…' Why do you think Tom whispers rather than speaking normally?

....

....

2 marks

4 'Tom's mind gave a jerk…' What does this phrase mean?

....

1 mark

1 What evidence is there that Tom's uncle and aunt follow a predictable routine?

1 mark

2 Which two pieces of evidence tell us that Tom is not in his own home?

2 marks

3 '…the house seemed to hold its breath…' How does this phrase support the idea that something important is about to happen?

2 marks

Total: _______ / 15 marks

Had a go ☐　　Getting there ☐　　Got it! ☐

Young Heroes: Inspirational Children From Around the World

George Matus

1998- DRONE ENGINEER   USA

When eleven-year-old George Matus and his family moved to Salt Lake City in Utah, USA, he found himself living in an enormous natural playground. Salt Lake City is surrounded by snow-capped mountains, and what better way to explore them than from way up in the sky? George bought a remote control (RC) helicopter and attached a camera to it. When he uploaded footage to YouTube, the helicopter's makers saw it and invited him to become a test pilot. The schoolboy had soon tested every RC aircraft, and drones became his passion.

But what exactly is a drone? Think of it as a tiny aircraft but without a pilot on board. Instead, it is operated from the ground by remote control. Not only are drones fun to fly but they're also a safer alternative to sending a person into a dangerous area, such as a battlefield or disaster zone.

George spent every spare moment flying and adapting drones but he soon grew frustrated. Most drones are designed for one job: some are built for racing, others to capture footage of the Earth from the clouds. Why couldn't a single drone do all these things? That's when George began creating his "wish list" for the perfect drone.

At sixteen, George won a grant from the Thiel Foundation, which invests in young entrepreneurs, to develop his drone. Several years later, he'd built Teal and Teal 2, the world's fastest battery-operated drones. Teal 1 and 2 can reach speeds of up to 137 kmh (85 mph). Best of all, they do every job on George's wish list.

Today, George is flying high. At eighteen, he became founder and chief executive of Teal Drones, while his dream drones are now being sold around the world. You could say that his idea really took off!

"Really find what interests you, and then it doesn't feel like work."

By Lula Bridgeport

1 What adjective is used to explain that the tops of the mountains are covered in snow?

....

1 mark

2 The author says George 'uploaded footage to YouTube'. What is another word for 'footage'?

....

1 mark

3 '…drones became his passion.' Circle the word below that is closest in meaning to 'passion'.

affection   **interest**   **enthusiasm**   **knowledge**

1 mark

4 '…flying and adapting drones…' Write down a word with a similar meaning to 'adapting'.

....

1 mark

1 '…an enormous natural playground…' Why do you think the writer describes George's new home in this way?

....

....

1 mark

2 Find one thing George's RC helicopter has in common with a drone.

....

1 mark

3 What is meant by George's 'wish-list'?

....

1 mark

4 '…his idea really took off!' What does this phrase mean?

....

....

1 mark

1 mark

Challenge 3

1 Why is it safer to send a drone into a dangerous situation?

1 mark

2 How do we know the helicopter makers were impressed by George's drone?

1 mark

3 Why do you think the Thiel Foundation gave George a grant?

2 marks

4 How do we know that George enjoys his work as founder and chief executive of Teal Drones?

2 marks

Total: _______ / 15 marks

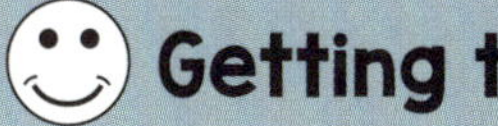 **Had a go**    **Getting there**   **Got it!**

41

The Sound Collector

A stranger called this morning
Dressed all in black and grey
Put every sound into a bag
And carried them away.

The whistling of the kettle
The turning of the lock
The purring of the kitten
The ticking of the clock

The popping of the toaster
The crunching of the flakes
When you spread the marmalade
The scraping sound it makes

The hissing of the frying-pan
The ticking of the grill
The bubbling of the bathtub
As it starts to fill

The drumming of the raindrops
On the window-pane
When you do the washing-up
The gurgle of the drain

The crying of the baby
The squeaking of the chair
The swishing of the curtain
The creaking of the stair

A stranger called this morning
He didn't leave his name
Left us only silence
Life will never be the same.

By Roger McGough

1 What word tells us that the poet does not know who the sound collector is?

1 mark

2 What object in the poem makes a whistling sound?

1 mark

3 Find two things in the poem that make a ticking sound.

2 marks

4 According to the poem, what did the sound collector leave behind?

1 mark

5 'On the window-pane...' What is the 'pane' of a window usually made of?

1 mark

1 'The turning of the lock...' What word could you use to describe the sound of a lock being turned?

1 mark

2 'The crunching of the flakes...' What are the 'flakes' in this line? How do you know?

2 marks

3 On what do you think marmalade is being spread? Give two reasons for your answer, based on the text.

3 marks

4 Why might a frying-pan make a 'hissing' sound?

....

1 mark

5 Alliteration is where two words close together start with the same sound. Find and copy an example from the fourth verse.

....

1 mark

Challenge 3

1 What does the stranger do in the first verse, and why is it odd?

....

....

2 marks

2 How do you think the narrator feels about living without all of the sounds? Give a reason for your answer.

....

....

2 marks

3 If this were to happen to you, which of the sounds mentioned would you miss the most, and why?

....

....

1 mark

Total: _______ / 19 marks

Had a go ☐   Getting there ☐   Got it! ☐

Amina's Voice

Something sharp pokes me in the rib.

"You should totally sign up for a solo," Soojin whispers from the seat behind me in music class.

I shake my head. The mere thought of singing in front of a crowd makes my stomach twist into knots.

"But you're such a good singer," Soojin insists.

I pause, enjoying the praise for a second. Soojin is the only one at school who knows I can sing, and she thinks I'm amazing at it. Every Tuesday we argue about the best contestant on *The Voice* and who deserves to advance to the next round. I can count on Soojin to end the conversation by saying that I'm better than most of the people on the show, and that I deserve to be on it someday. But what she doesn't consider is that if by some miracle I was standing in front of the judges and live studio audience, I wouldn't be able to croak out a word. I shake my head again.

"Come on, Amina. Just try it." Soojin is a little louder now.

"Girls, is that chatter about you volunteering?" Ms. Holly stared at us from the front of the classroom with her eyebrows raised.

"Ouch!" I yelp. It's Soojin's pencil in my side again.

"Is that a yes, Amina? Should I sign you up for a solo for the concert?" Ms. Holly asks. "How about one of the Motown pieces from the 1970s?"

I sink lower in my chair as everyone stares at me and stumble over my words. "Um, no, thank you. I'll just stay in the chorus," I finally manage to mutter.

"Okay." Ms Holly shrugs, a frown clouding her face until Julie Zawacki, waving her hand like an overenthusiastic first grader, distracts her. Julie always wants the spotlight and tends to sing extremely loudly. It's as if she thinks volume makes up for her lack of pitch. I always wonder how the math class next door gets any work done whenever Julie starts belting. But I still wish I had even half the guts she does.

"Remember, we've only got two months to prepare for the Winter Choral Concert. This is a big deal, guys," Ms. Holly calls out as the bell rings and we file out for lunch.

By Hena Khan

1. 'You should totally sign up for a solo…' What is a 'solo'?

....

1 mark

2. '…we argue about the best contestant…' Circle the word below which is closest in meaning to 'contestant'.

actor   **celebrity**   **competitor**   **judge**

1 mark

3. '…a frown clouding her face…' Why do you think the author has used the word 'clouding'?

....

....

1 mark

4. What class takes place in the room next door?

....

1 mark

1. 'Something sharp pokes me in the rib.' What is it that pokes Amina in the ribs in the first line of the text? How do you know?

....

....

2 marks

2. 'Julie always wants the spotlight…' What does this suggest about Julie?

....

1 mark

3. '…whenever Julie starts belting.' What does the word 'belting' in this phrase mean?

....

1 mark

4. '…stumble over my words.' What does this phrase tell you about Amina?

....

1 mark

5. Soojin 'whispers' to Amina at the start of the text. Why does she whisper?

....

1 mark

1 Why does Amina's 'stomach twist into knots'?

2 marks

2 '…I wouldn't be able to croak out a word.' If Amina can sing, why would it sound like she was croaking if she were to sing for the judges?

2 marks

3 Find two differences between Amina and Julie.

2 marks

4 Do you think Amina will end up singing a solo in the Winter Choral Concert? Give a reason for your answer.

1 mark

Total: _______ / 17 marks

Had a go

Getting there

Got it!

Lauren Child

Children's Laureate 2017–19

So Where Do You Get Your Ideas From?

For me, ideas come from everywhere: in a supermarket queue, out of the window, a sentence overheard, a book read, a football kicked, etc. I have been writing things and illustrating them since I was a young child. Back then, I was more interested in the drawing, but it seemed important to have a narrative to work to. As a teenager I wrote comics in class with my friends. I liked that way of telling a story, where the images are what you read and the words are secondary, there just to add detail and help explain things more clearly.

After I left school I wrote a children's picture book with a friend. Surprisingly, a publisher was actually interested in it, but we were young, easily distracted and unprepared for the work it takes to produce a finished book. Once I'd left college I started to take things more seriously and wrote many picture-book ideas, but I just couldn't seem to come up with anything authentic and original.

My ideas were rejected over and over again, and I was given a lot of criticism and advice, not all of it useful. At the time it was very tough, although looking back it was a useful experience: I had to be determined and resilient, and the time I spent struggling helped me work out what it was I wanted to say and find my own way of saying it.

I thought back to the things I used to write when I was a child, which were always personal and often about my own family – so I wrote about a family and a middle child, a seven year-old called Clarice Bean. Everything was told from her point of view, in her voice.

I began to write and draw at the same time, just like I had when I was a child.

I used my experiences of growing up in a busy household, remembering the funny and peculiar things that happened.

Flights of Fancy: Stories, Pictures and Inspiration from Ten Children's Laureates
by various authors

1 '...writing things and illustrating them...' What does 'illustrating' mean?

1 mark

2 What is another word for 'narrative'?

1 mark

3 What is another word for 'images'?

1 mark

4 Where did Child study after she left school?

1 mark

5 '...a sentence overheard...' What does 'overheard' mean?

1 mark

Challenge 2

1 The extract begins with a list of some of the things that give Child ideas for her stories. Find something else that gives her ideas, mentioned in another part of the text.

1 mark

2 According to Child, what are more important in comics – the words or the pictures?

1 mark

3 How do we know that Child had no idea of the work involved in writing a book?

1 mark

4 Find something in the text that Child did as a child and now does again.

1 mark

1 'Surprisingly, a publisher was actually interested in it…' Why do you think Child has used the word 'surprisingly' here?

2 marks

2 What was Child's response to being rejected? How do we know it worked?

2 marks

3 How have Child's thoughts about being rejected changed over time?

2 marks

4 What evidence is there in the text to support the idea that the Clarice Bean stories might be about funny things that happened to Child herself?

2 marks

Total: _______ / 17 marks

 **Had a go**    **Getting there**   😃 **Got it!**

Cat

You need your Cat.
When you slump down
All tired and flat
With too much town

With too many lifts
Too many floors
Too many neon-lit
Corridors

Too many people
Telling you what
You just must do
And what you must not

With too much headache
Video glow
Too many answers
You will never know

Then stroke the Cat
That warms your knee
You'll find her purr
Is a battery

For into your hands
Will flow the powers
Of the beasts who ignore
These ways of ours

And you'll be refreshed
Through the Cat on your lap
With a Leopard's yawn
And a Tiger's nap.

By Ted Hughes

Challenge 1

1. 'When you slump down…' Circle the word below that is closest in meaning to the word 'slump'.

   sag   **fail**   **climb**   **rest**

   1 mark

2. Write another word similar in meaning to 'corridors'.

   1 mark

3. 'Of the beasts who ignore…' What is another word for 'beasts'?

   1 mark

4. '…a Tiger's nap.' What type of sleep is a 'nap'?

   1 mark

5. 'Video glow…' What is another word for 'glow'?

   1 mark

Challenge 2

1. 'All tired and flat…' What do you think the poet means by 'flat' in this line?

   1 mark

2. Find two examples of technology that might make someone tired.

   2 marks

3. According to the poem, how might other people make someone tired?

   1 mark

4. Why does the poem suggest that cats are not made tired by the same things as people?

   1 mark

5. 'Then stroke the Cat / That warms your knee…' Find and copy words from somewhere else in the poem that describe where the cat sits.

   1 mark

1 Why does the poet say the cat's purr is a 'battery'?

2 marks

2 How does the poem suggest the 'powers' will pass from the cat into the person?

2 marks

3 Why do you think the writer has mentioned a leopard and a tiger?

2 marks

Total: _______ / 17 marks

 **Had a go**    **Getting there**    **Got it!**

Progress Test 2

***The Star Outside my Window* by Onjali Rauf**

I've always wanted to be a Star Hunter.

Everyone else calls them astronomers, but I think 'Star Hunter' sounds much better, so that's what I'm going to call myself. But I'm not going to be the kind of star hunter that looks for old stars. I want to find the brand new ones – the ones that have only just been born and are searching for the people they've left behind. I read in a library book once that stars can burn for millions and billions and even trillions of years. I hope that's true, because there's one star I don't ever want to stop burning. I don't know where it is yet, but I know it's out there, waiting for me to find it.

Back in my real house where I lived with Mum and Dad, I had three whole shelves of books in my bedroom, and at least half of them were all about stars and space travel. The walls and ceiling were covered with posters and glow-in-the-dark stars that I'd begged Mum and Dad to get me. But the best thing in my room was my special star globe which sat right next to my bed. From far away, it looked like a globe of the world – but it wasn't. It was a globe of the night sky, and instead of countries and oceans, it lit up with all the different star constellations you could ever think of. There was a different constellation every time you switched it on, and I knew all of them off by heart. That's why new stars will be easy for me to spot when I'm a star hunter – if you know a picture off by heart, it's easy to tell when something about it is different.

1. **What does an 'astronomer' do?**

1 mark

2. **Name two places where the narrator finds information about space.**

2 marks

3. **What do you think would be on the posters on the narrator's bedroom wall? Give a reason for your answer based on the text.**

2 marks

4. **Why do you think the narrator wanted glow-in-the-dark stars on their bedroom ceiling?**

1 mark

5. **Find and copy the word that tells you that the narrator had to persuade their parents to buy glow-in-the-dark stars.**

1 mark

6. **The narrator has a star globe. What shape is a globe? Circle your answer.**

cube   sphere   pyramid   cone

1 mark

7. **How do we know that the narrator's star globe doesn't always look the same?**

1 mark

8. **What does it mean if you learn something 'off by heart'?**

1 mark

9. **How do we know that the narrator looks at their star globe a lot?**

2 marks

10. What do you think an 'illustrator' does?

1 mark

11. Do you think many people in the 1600s had 'favourite' insects? Give a reason for your answer based on the text.

1 mark

12. What did Maria discover about caterpillars?

1 mark

13. Which word shows that Maria's life changed to a large degree when she left Germany for Holland.

1 mark

14. How many children did Maria have?

1 mark

15. Where is Suriname?

1 mark

16. What does the phrase 'braved its rainforests' suggest about Maria's visit to the Suriname rainforests?

1 mark

17. In which years were Maria's books published?

1 mark

18. Which phrase shows that Maria's second book was a success?

1 mark

19. What specifically about Maria's illustrations amazes people today?

1 mark

Total: _______ / 22 marks

The Butterfly Lion

That night he made up his mind what had to be done. He waited until he heard his father's deep breathing next door. Then, with his white lion at his heels, he crept downstairs in his pyjamas, took down his father's rifle from the rack and stepped out into the night. The compound gate yawned open noisily when he pushed it, but then they were out, out and running free. Bertie had not thought of the dangers around him, only that he must get as far from home as he could before he did it.

The lion padded along beside him, stopping every now and again to sniff the air. A clump of trees became a herd of elephants wandering towards them out of the dawn. Bertie ran for it. He knew how elephants hated lions. He ran and ran till his legs could run no more. As the sun came up over the **veld** he climbed to the top of a **kopje** and sat down, his arm round the lion's neck. The time had come.

"Be wild now," he whispered. "You've got to be wild. Don't come home. Don't ever come home. They'll put you behind bars. You hear what I'm saying? All my life I'll think of you, I promise I will. I won't ever forget you." And he buried his head in the lion's neck and heard the greeting groan from deep inside him. He stood up. "I'm going now," he said. "Don't follow me. Please don't follow me." And Bertie clambered down off the kopje and walked away.

When he looked back, the lion was still sitting there watching him; but then he stood up, yawned, stretched, licked his lips and sprang down after him. Bertie shouted at him, but he kept coming. He threw sticks. He threw stones. Nothing worked. The lion would stop, but then as soon as Bertie walked on, he simply followed at a safe distance.

"Go back!" Bertie yelled, "you stupid, stupid lion! I hate you! I hate you! Go back!" But the lion kept loping after him whatever he did, whatever he said.

There was only one thing for it. He didn't want to do it, but he had to. With tears filling his eyes and his mouth, he lifted the rifle to his shoulder and fired over the lion's head. At once the lion turned tail and scampered away through the veld. Bertie fired again. He watched till he could see him no more, and then turned for home.

By Michael Morpurgo

Veld: open grassland in South Africa

Kopje: a small hill

1 What is unusual about the appearance of the lion?

____

1 mark

2 '…out of the dawn.' What time of day is dawn?

____

1 mark

3 '…clambered down…' Write another word similar in meaning to 'clambered'.

____

1 mark

4 '…the lion kept loping after him…' Circle the word below that is closest in meaning to 'loping'.

creeping   **stalking**   **striding**   **wading**

1 mark

Challenge 2

1 What does his father's 'deep breathing' tell Bertie?

____

1 mark

2 'Bertie had not thought of the dangers around him' so why do you think he takes his father's rifle with him?

____

1 mark

3 'The compound gate yawned open noisily…' What does this phrase mean?

____

____

2 marks

4 Why do you think elephants hate lions?

____

1 mark

5 What does the phrase 'put you behind bars' mean?

____

1 mark

1 'A clump of trees became a herd of elephants…' What do you think is happening at this point in the story?

____

____

2 marks

2 Bertie tells the lion to 'Be wild now'. What does this suggest about how the lion had been living up to this point?

____

1 mark

3 '…you stupid, stupid lion! I hate you!' Do you think Bertie really hates the lion? Give a reason for your answer.

____

____

2 marks

4 'With tears filling his eyes and his mouth…' Why do you think Bertie is crying at this point in the story?

____

____

2 marks

5 What do you think might happen next in the story?

____

____

1 mark

Total: _______ / 18 marks

 **Had a go**    **Getting there**     **Got it!**

Peru

Pop. size 30,375,603 (42nd)

Landmass (km²) 1,285,216 (19th)

Life Expectancy 73.23 (105th)

Peru is one of the world's most fascinating countries. Contained within its borders are so many natural and man-made wonders that is has become the most popular South American destination for backpackers.

If you want to see coast, mountains, rainforests and deserts in one go – Peru is the place.

PADDINGTON

The world-famous teddy bear, Paddington, may be a resident of London now, but author Michael Bond's furry creation is actually from 'darkest Peru'.

THE GRANDEST CANYON

Cotahuasi Canyon, near the city of Arequipa, is the deepest canyon in the world. It is 3,354m (11,000ft) deep. That means you could stack 11 Eiffel Towers on top of each other, and they still wouldn't reach the top!

MASHCO-PIRO

It is said that there are more than 70 uncontacted tribes in the Amazon jungle. The Mashco-Piro are one of Peru's, and to this day they still thrive in the far west of the Peruvian Amazon, remaining separate from the modern world. It is thought that only 250 people of their kind survive.

POTATOES

When Spanish conquistadors defeated the Inca Empire, the first thing they brought back to Europe was the potato. Peru's Inca Indians first grew the potato thousands of years ago. The ancient Inca Indians valued the potato not only as a food, but as a measure of time. Units of time were related to how long it took a potato to boil.

PIGGIES

To many, guinea pigs are adorable pets. To Peruvians they are a tasty treat! More than 60 million guinea pigs are eaten each year in Peru. Could you eat one?

NAZCA LINES

One of the world's greatest mysteries, the Nazca Lines are a collection of giant pictures scratched on the floor of the Nazca desert. Created around 2,000 years ago, there are over 70 animals and plants drawn into the red desert landscape, including sharks, hummingbirds, spiders, lizards and whales.

BRIDGE OF EGGS

Puente de Piedra (the Bridge of Stone) is, unsurprisingly, made of stone. But rather more surprisingly it's also made of eggs! Over 10,000 eggs were used to stick the bricks together. It's still standing 400 years later!

WONDER OF THE WORLD

Machu Picchu is an unbelievable ruin of a forgotten Inca city. Perched in the cloud forests of Peru, the city's ruins, containing a palace and other sacred sites, were rediscovered in 1911.

The Travel Book: A Journey Through Every Country in the World by Lonely Planet Kids

1 '…one of the world's most fascinating countries.' Write another word similar in meaning to 'fascinating'.

____

1 mark

2 '…natural and man-made wonders…' What is another word for 'wonders'?

____

1 mark

3 '…they still thrive…' Circle the word below that is closest in meaning to 'thrive'.

farm   **prosper**   **struggle**   **hide**

1 mark

4 'When Spanish conquistadors defeated the Inca Empire…' Circle the word below that is closest in meaning to 'defeated'.

destroyed   **fought**   **chased**   **beat**

1 mark

5 How were the pictures in the Nazca Desert made?

____

1 mark

Challenge 2

1 Which two sections of the text give information about food?

____

1 mark

2 Why do you think a lot of people want to visit Peru?

____

1 mark

3 Find and copy one natural and one man-made place a visitor to Peru might want to see.

Natural place	a)
Man-made place	b)

2 marks

4 Do you think 'Bridge of Eggs' is a good title for the section about the Puente de Piedra? Give a reason for your answer.

....

1 mark

5 Find two pieces of information about the Inca from the text.

....

2 marks

Challenge 3

1 Give a reason why nobody is sure how many members of the Mashco-Piro tribe there are.

....

1 mark

2 What evidence is there in the text that eggs can make a good building material?

....

....

2 marks

3 Can you think of a reason why the Nazca Lines might be described as 'mysteries'?

....

1 mark

4 What does the word 'perched' suggest about Machu Picchu?

....

2 marks

Total: _______ / 18 marks

 **Had a go**  **Getting there**  **Got it!** 

Sun and Flowers

The spring is coming! hear it blow!
The rain and wind have cleared the snow;
And I am going to play my fill
With sunlight on the windy hill.

And I am going to laugh and run,
And be the comrade of the sun;
And, like the wildflowers, wink my eyes
At him and at the springtime skies.

And I am going to leap and shout
And toss my hair and arms about,
And fill my soul with sunshine as
The blossoms do and waving grass.

And I am going to dance and sing
And match the swallow on the wing,
And put my arms about each tree,
And kiss it as the sun does me.

And I am going to lie face down
Upon the hillside, far from town,
And hug it as the sunlight does,
And watch the pussy-willows fuzz.

I wish I was as big and bright
As is the sunlight: then I might
Hold all the hillside in my joy
But I am just a little boy.

And I am only sweet and small
As are the wildflowers, that is all,
So mother says; and thus you see
The sun can get ahead of me.

Blow wind and rain! and sweep away
The snow and sleet of yesterday!
And bring the sunlight and the flowers
And all the laughing springtime hours.

By Madison Julius Cawein

1 Which part of the body is the poet comparing the flowers to?

1 mark

2 '…fill my soul with sunshine…' What does this suggest about how the arrival of spring might change how the narrator is feeling?

1 mark

3 According to the poem, how is the narrator similar to a wildflower?

1 mark

4 How do you think the narrator of the poem feels about the winter? Give a reason for your answer.

2 marks

5 How do you think the spring might be different in the town mentioned in the poem?

1 mark

Total: _______ / 16 marks

 **Had a go**    **Getting there**   **Got it!**

The Beast of Buckingham Palace

It was noon, and the sky was black.

There had been darkness over the kingdom for half a century. For, many years before, the people of the Earth had not taken care of their home.

They had **burned** down all the forests, reducing every last tree to ash.

They had **pumped** the rivers, lakes and seas full of waste, killing all the fish.

They had dug **deeper** and **deeper** under the ground for oil, until the planet was hollow to its core.

Eventually, the Earth took its **revenge**.

The ice caps of the Arctic and Antarctic **melted**. The floods were so mighty that whole countries became **submerged** underwater.

Violent earthquakes **shook** entire cities to the ground. All that was left behind were **piles and piles of rubble**.

Volcanoes **erupted**, pumping billions of tonnes of ash into the air. Without the sunlight, the crops **withered and died**. Nothing could grow.

The kingdom was plunged into an **ETERNAL WINTER**.

It was the only world Alfred knew. He was already twelve years old, but had never, ever seen sunlight. Often, he dreamed how it must have been to feel the sun on your face, or run through a field of tall grass, or swim in a sunlit sea. But it was just that, a dream.

The boy had seen pictures of the sun in books and marvelled at it. A perfect circle of gold. Now the moon and stars had become invisible too. Alfred would spend hours and hours imagining how the night sky must have looked with a thousand little lights twinkling through the blackness.

He was one of those children who liked nothing more than being alone with his imagination. In truth, he had little choice, having been sickly his whole life. Soon after he was born, he became ill. As a baby, Alfred had not been expected to survive, but survive he did.

Just.

The child was as pale as snow and as thin as dust. He wore thick glasses to aid his poor eyesight. Often Alfred was so weak he had to stay in bed all day. Thank goodness all around him were piles and piles of books. Books, books and more **books**. Books about animals. Books about space. Books about trees. Books about dinosaurs. Books about **books**.

Books about history were his absolute favourite.

The trouble was that there was a strict curfew in the building where Alfred lived. Night was the most dangerous time. That was when there was most chance of an attack from the outside. Lights had to be out at eight o'clock sharp. By order of the King.

By David Walliams

1 '…there was a strict curfew…' What is a curfew?

1 mark

2 'The floods were so mighty…' Write another word similar in meaning to 'mighty'.

1 mark

3 '…the crops withered…' Circle the word that is closest in meaning to 'withered'.

stunted   grew   wilted   starved

1 mark

4 '…an **ETERNAL WINTER**.' Circle the word that is closest in meaning to 'eternal'.

cold   dark   everlasting   short

1 mark

1 'There had been darkness over the kingdom for half a century.' How many years are there in half a century?

1 mark

2 Give two reasons why you think the writer has made some of the words in the first half of the extract bold.

2 marks

3 '…there was a strict curfew…' Find another piece of evidence in the text that supports the idea that there was no flexibility about when Alfred had to turn off his light.

1 mark

4 Find two different places in the text where ash is mentioned.

2 marks

5 Give one reason why the writer describes the picture of the sun as 'A perfect circle of gold'.

1 mark

1 Why was there no sunlight?

1 mark

2 '…a thousand little lights twinkling through the blackness.' What are the lights the text refers to? Give a reason for your answer.

2 marks

3 Give two reasons why the phrase 'as pale as snow' reinforces the idea that Alfred is 'sickly'.

2 marks

4 Find and copy two pieces of evidence in the text that show that Alfred likes to read.

2 marks

5 Why might the curfew have been a problem for a child who loved to read?

2 marks

Total: _______ / 20 marks

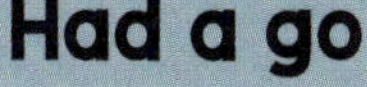 **Had a go**    **Getting there**    **Got it!**

Wind and Water Power

The two main natural sources of motion come from the flow of water through Earth's ocean and rivers, and the rush of winds that blow across the planet. Scientists are using these sources to make electricity.

Gravity, coming from the moon and the sun, lifts the ocean's water over coastlines twice a day and then pulls it back again. Earth's gravity is also pulling the water in rivers and streams down through valleys and over waterfalls until it reaches the sea.

Winds are caused by the air being spread unevenly over the planet. The sun heats some of the air, making it bunch together in areas of high pressure. The air then spreads out into areas with lower pressure. That spreading out is what creates the flow of wind. Finally, wind blowing over the ocean causes ripples on the surface of the water. These build into the mighty waves that crash against the shore. We've been harnessing these natural motions for centuries, and today we rely on them more and more as a source of clean, pollution-free energy.

SAILING AWAY

The first wind-powered machines were sailboats. The earliest sails date from more than 8,000 years ago and we still use them today. A sail moves a ship by catching the wind. Wind pushes on the back of the sail, transferring some of the wind's momentum to the sail and the boat, moving the craft forward. Expert sailors learn to position sails at different angles to capture the right amount of wind for speed and direction. The fastest sail-powered boats can travel more than 60 miles an hour (100 km/h), which is faster than most engine-powered vessels.

WINDMILLS

Sails are not just used at sea. Simple windmills use sails arranged around a wheel to catch the wind. The force of the wind makes the wheel spin. This spinning motion was originally used to turn heavy stone wheels inside windmills that ground grain into flour. A modern windmill, or wind turbine, uses the spinning motion to generate electricity. The turbine's blades are not cloth sails but solid wing-shaped fins, often made of aluminium. They convert the smooth motion of the wind flowing over them into a sideways spinning motion that produces electricity.

BLOCKING A RIVER

Rivers have long been used as a source of power. Ancient Greeks invented waterwheels to use in rivers 2,200 years ago. Large wheels with blades or scoops all around them were pushed by the flow of the river water, making the wheel spin. Modern waterwheels are inside hydroelectric dams. The term "hydroelectric" means converting water power into electricity. The dam is a sturdy concrete barrier that blocks the normal flow of a river. A deep lake builds up behind the dam, and its water is then channelled through fan-like waterwheels built deep inside the dam. These waterwheels help to power 10 percent of the world's electricity.

Science Encyclopedia: Atom Smashing, Food Chemistry, Animals, Space and More! by National Geographic Kids

1. '…sources of motion…' What is another word for 'motion'?

   ....

   1 mark

2. '…causes ripples on the surface…' What is another word for 'ripples'?

   ....

   1 mark

3. '…harnessing these natural motions…' Circle the word below that is closest in meaning to 'harnessing'.

   slowing   **exploiting**   **finding**   **powering**

   1 mark

4. '…a sturdy concrete barrier…' What is another word for 'sturdy'?

   ....

   1 mark

1. According to the text, is there more air, or less air, in areas of high pressure?

   ....

   1 mark

2. Apart from being powered by 'clean' energy, how can sailboats be better than boats powered by engines?

   ....

   1 mark

3. According to the text, what skill do good sailors need?

   ....

   1 mark

4. '…originally used to turn heavy stone wheels…' What does the adjective 'heavy' suggest about how easy it is to grind grain into flour?

   ....

   1 mark

5. Which was invented first, the sailboat or the water wheel?

   ....

   1 mark

1 Name two roles that the sun plays in making electricity.

2 marks

2 What would happen if the air were spread evenly over the surface of the Earth? Explain your answer, based on the text.

2 marks

3 Find and copy the phrase that shows that using wind and water power is not a new idea.

1 mark

4 Describe one difference between Ancient Greek and modern waterwheels.

1 mark

5 Why do dams need to be 'sturdy'?

1 mark

Total: _______ / 16 marks

 **Had a go**    **Getting there**   **Got it!**

The Magic of the Brain

Such a sight I saw:
An eight-sided kite surging up into a cloud
Its eight tails streaming out as if they were one.
It lifted my heart as starlight lifts the head
Such a sight I saw.

And such a sound I heard.
One bird through dim winter light as the day was closing
Poured out a song suddenly from an empty tree.
It cleared my head as water refreshes the skin
Such a sound I heard.

Such a smell I smelled:
A mixture of roses and coffee, of green leaf and warmth.
It took me to gardens and summer and cities abroad,
Memories of meetings as if my past friends were here
Such a smell I smelled.

Such a soft fur I felt.
It wrapped me around, soothing my winter-cracked skin,
Not gritty or stringy or sweaty but silkily warm
As my animal slept on my lap, and we both breathed
    content
Such soft fur I felt.

Such food I tasted:
Smooth-on-tongue-soup, and juicy crackling of meat,
Greens like fresh fields, sweet-on-your-palate peas,
Jellies and puddings and fragrance of fruit they are
    made from
Such good food I tasted.

Such a world comes in:
Far world of the sky to breathe in through your nose
Near world you feel underfoot as you walk on the land.
Through your eyes and your ears and your mouth and
    your brilliant brain
Such a world comes in.

By Jenny Joseph

1 '…surging up into a cloud…' Circle the word below that is closest in meaning to 'surging'.

fleeing **floating** **drifting** **rushing**

1 mark

2 '…water refreshes the skin…' What is another word for 'refreshes'?

1 mark

3 What are the 'Jellies and puddings' in the poem made from?

1 mark

4 '…your brilliant brain…' What is another word for 'brilliant', as it is used in this line?

1 mark

Challenge 2

1 'It lifted my heart…' What does this phrase mean?

1 mark

2 '…as the day was closing…' What time of day do you think the poet is referring to?

1 mark

3 'It took me to gardens and summer and cities abroad…' Do you think the smell actually took the poet to another place? Explain your answer.

2 marks

4 '…my animal slept on my lap…' What type of animal do you think 'my animal' might be? Give a reason for your answer.

2 marks

5 'Greens like fresh fields...' Why do you think the poet compares the vegetables to 'fresh fields'?

2 marks

Challenge 3

1 In what season does the poem take place? Find two pieces of evidence from different parts of the poem.

2 marks

2 '...as starlight lifts the head...' How or why might starlight lift someone's head?

2 marks

3 'Poured out a song...' What does this phrase suggest about what the birdsong sounded like?

2 marks

4 According to the poem, which of the senses can bring back memories?

1 mark

5 'Such a world comes in...' What do you think the poet means by this line?

1 mark

Total: _______ / 20 marks

 **Had a go**    **Getting there**    **Got it!**

81

When Hitler Stole Pink Rabbit

Papa had reserved rooms for them in the best hotel in Zurich. It had a revolving door and thick carpets and lots of gold everywhere. As it was still only ten o'clock in the morning they ate another breakfast while they talked about everything that had happened since Papa had left Berlin.

At first there seemed endless things to tell him, but after a while they found it was nice just being together without saying anything at all. While Anna and Max ate their way through two different kinds of croissants and four different types of jam, Mama and Papa sat smiling at each other. Every so often they would remember something and Papa would say, 'Did you manage to bring the books?' or Mama would say, 'The paper rang and they'd like an article from you this week if possible.' But they would relapse back into their contented, smiling silence.

At last Max drank the last of his hot chocolate, wiped the last crumbs of croissant off his lips and said, 'What shall we do now?'

Somehow nobody had thought.

After a moment Papa said, 'Let's go and look at Zurich'.

They decided first of all to go to the top of a hill overlooking the city. The hill was so steep that you had to go by funicular – a kind of lift on wheels that went straight up at an alarming angle. Anna had never been in one before and spent her time between excitement at the experience and anxious scrutiny of the cable for signs of fraying. From the top of the hill you could see Zurich clustered below at one end of an enormous blue lake. It was so big that the town seemed quite small by comparison, and its far end was hidden by mountains. Steamers, which looked like toys from this height, were making their way round the edge of the lake, stopping at each of the villages scattered along the shores and then moving on to the next. The sun was shining and made it all look very inviting.

'Can anyone go on those steamers?' asked Max. It was just what Anna had been going to ask.

'Would you like to go?' said Papa. 'So you shall – this afternoon.'

Lunch was splendid, at a restaurant with a glassed-in terrace overlooking the lake below, but Anna could not each much. Her head was feeling swimmy, probably from getting up so early, she thought, and though her nose had stopped running, her throat was sore.

'Are you all right?' asked Mama anxiously.

'Oh yes!' said Anna, thinking of the steamer trip in the afternoon. Anyway, she was sure it was just tiredness.

By Judith Kerr

1 '…contented, smiling silence.' What is another word for 'contented'?

1 mark

2 '…anxious scrutiny of the cable…' Circle the word below that is closest in meaning to 'scrutiny'.

clutching   **fear**   **examination**   **excitement**

1 mark

3 Which was bigger, the city of Zurich or the lake?

1 mark

4 Find and copy the adjective that tells you that the lunch was excellent.

1 mark

Challenge 2

1 Find and copy two details about the hotel that support the idea that it is 'the best hotel in Zurich'.

2 marks

2 Find and copy the phrase that tells you the children had already eaten that morning.

1 mark

3 Why was Anna worried about the funicular cable fraying?

2 marks

4 What job do you think Papa does? Give a reason for your answer.

2 marks

5 '…you could see Zurich clustered below…' How does the word 'clustered' support the idea that the streets of Zurich are closely packed together?

____

1 mark

Challenge 3

1 Why did the steamers look like toys?

____

1 mark

2 Why does Max ask if anyone can go on the steamers?

____

1 mark

3 Why do you think the steamers stopped at the villages around the lake?

____

1 mark

4 How do you think Mama and Papa felt to be together again? Give a reason for your answer, based on the text.

____

2 marks

5 What do you think will happen to Anna next? Give a reason for your answer, based on the text.

____

____

2 marks

Total: _______ / 19 marks

😐 **Had a go** ☐   🙂 **Getting there** ☐   😄 **Got it!** ☐

Progress Test 3

The Sun is huge compared to even the biggest of the planets, Jupiter, and it contains 99.8 per cent of the Solar System's entire mass. At nearly 1.4 million km (870,000 miles) wide, the Sun is ten times wider than Jupiter and over 1,000 times more massive. Yet even Jupiter is gigantic compared to Earth. The Solar System's eight planets form two distinct groups. The inner planets – Mercury, Venus, Earth, and Mars – are solid balls of rock and metal. In contrast, the outer planets are gas giants – enormous, swirling globes made mostly of hydrogen and helium.

The Sun's family

The Solar System is a vast disc of material over 30 billion km (19 billion miles) across, with the Sun at its centre. Most of it is empty space, but scattered throughout are countless solid objects bound to the Sun by gravity and orbiting (travelling around) it, mostly in the same direction. The biggest objects are almost perfectly round and are called planets. There are eight of them, ranging from the small rocky planet Mercury to gigantic Jupiter. The Solar System also has hundreds of moons and dwarf planets, millions of asteroids, and possibly millions or billions of comets.

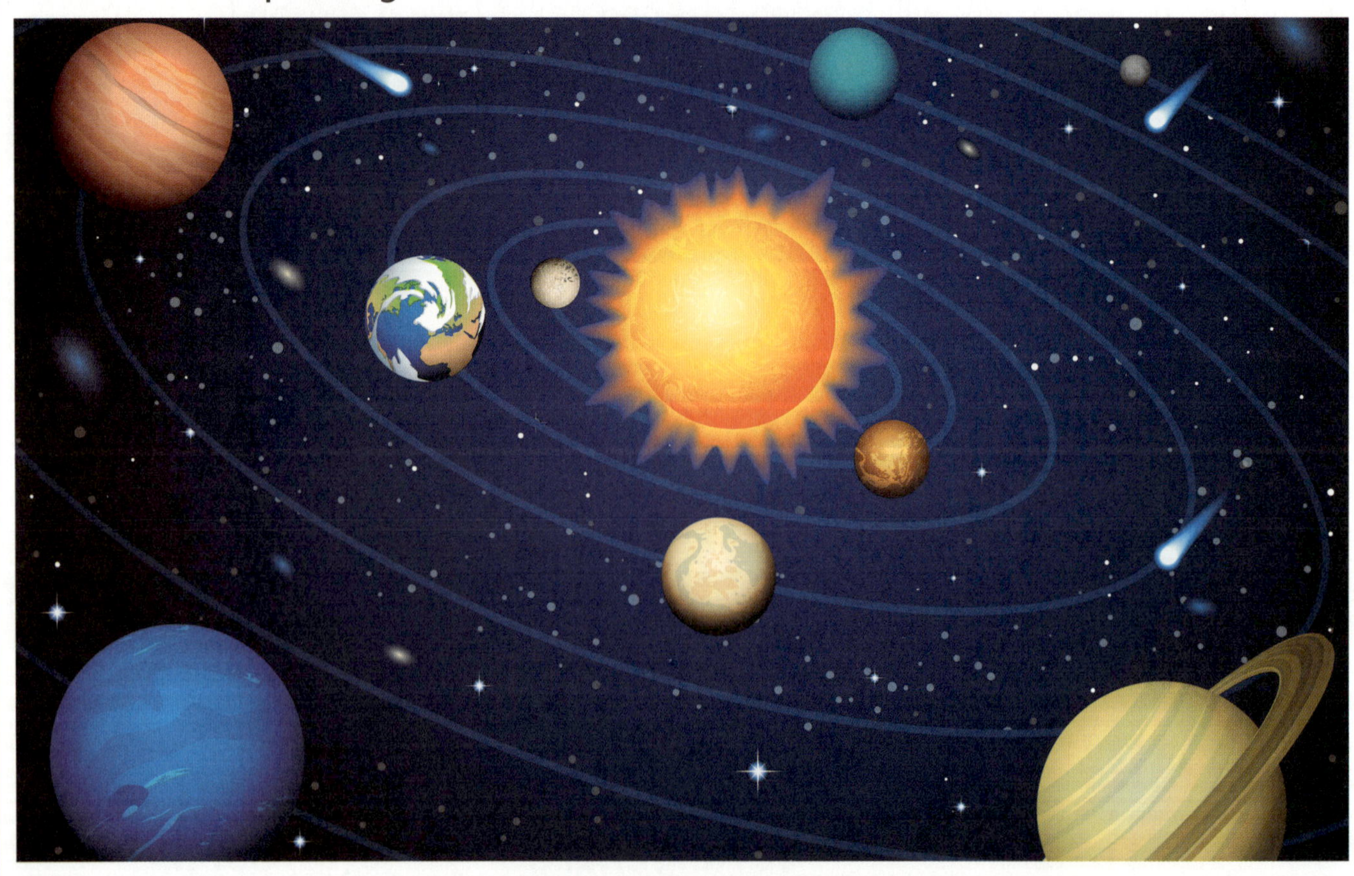

1. '...ten times wider than Jupiter...' Circle the word below that is closest in meaning to 'wider'.

   further   heavier   broader   taller

1 mark

2. '...two distinct groups.' Write another word similar in meaning to 'distinct'.

1 mark

3. 'The Sun is huge...' Write down four adjectives used in the text with a similar meaning to 'huge'.

4 marks

4. How are the inner and outer planets in the solar system different?

1 mark

5. Find and copy two gases named in the text.

2 marks

6. 'The Solar System is a vast disc...' Write down something in the everyday world that is shaped like a disc.

1 mark

7. If you were to cut Venus in half, what would you find inside?

1 mark

8. '...possibly millions or billions of comets.' What does the word 'possibly' suggest about how much we understand about the Solar System?

1 mark

***Look at all those monkeys* by Spike Milligan**

Look at all those monkeys
Jumping in their cage.
Why don't they all go out to work
And earn a decent wage?

*How can you say such silly things
Are you a son of mine?
Imagine monkeys travelling on
The Morden–Edgware line!*

But what about the Pekinese!
They have an allocation.
'Don't travel during Peke hour,'
It says on every station.

*My Gosh, you're right, my clever boy,
I never thought of that!*
And so they left the monkey house,
While an elephant raised his hat.

9. '...earn a decent wage?' What is a 'wage'?

....

1 mark

10. Where do you think the poem is set?

1 mark

11. Why are some parts of the poem in italics?

....

1 mark

12. *'Imagine monkeys travelling on / The Morden–Edgware line!'*
**What kind of line do you think the Morden–Edgware line is?
Give a reason for your answer.**

2 marks

13. **'Don't travel during Peke hour…' In this line, the word 'Peke' is
an example of word play and has been used instead of the word
'peak'. What would travelling during 'peak hour' mean?**

1 mark

14. **Why do you think people would be advised not to travel at
this time?**

1 mark

15. **What do you think the monkey house is?**

1 mark

16. **How does the parent's opinion of their son change during
the poem?**

2 marks

17. **'While an elephant raised his hat.' How does this line support
the idea that this is a nonsense poem?**

1 mark

18. *'My Gosh…'* **What do these words suggest the speaker is feeling
at this point in the poem?**

1 mark

Total: _______ / 24 marks

Answers

1.

huge	massive	enormous
angry	furious	raging
afraid	terrified	frightened

[6]

2. Answers will vary, e.g. castle, witch, princess. [3]
3. Answers will vary, e.g. robot, spaceship, alien. [3]
4. Answers will vary, e.g. ship, parrot, treasure. [3]
5. ugly [1] 6. a scream [1] 7. it disappeared [1]
8. nimble [1] 9. rapidly [1] 10. a made-up story [1]
11. Accept any one of: information, explanation, instruction, autobiography, biography, report writing. [1] 12. fiction [1] 13. non-fiction [1]
14.

Contents page	Alphabetical list of topics with their page numbers, found at the back of the book.
Index	Numbers on each page, to help you find the right page.
Glossary	List of chapters or sections with their page numbers, found at the front of the book.
Page numbers	Alphabetical list of words and their meanings, usually found at the back of the book. [4]

15. fiction [1] 16. The title mentions dragons which are made-up creatures. [2] 17. Accept any three from: strawberry, blackberry, gooseberry, raspberry. [1]
18. Yes, because he uses the word 'Deeeelicious'. [1]
19. 'a multi-topping pizza' [1] 20. non-fiction [1]
21. It gives factual information about ancient Egypt. [1]
22. Accept any word with a similar meaning to 'gloopy', e.g. messy, sticky. [1] 23. Accept any word with a similar meaning to 'wealthy', e.g. rich, prosperous. [1]
24. To draw attention to them. [1] 25. No [1]

26.

shell	smell
slap	lap
shore	more
flows	toes

[1]

27. Any one of: 'I can smell the salty sea'; 'I can hear the slap of the waves'; 'I can feel once more the tickling tide' [1]
28. 'salty' [1] 29. Yes, because they have kept the shell and use it to remember the sensations they experienced there. [1] 30. a) True, b) False, c) True [3] 31. He could not stop thinking. [1] 32. 12 [1] 33. blackness [1]
34. scraped loudly, racket [2] 35. electricity [1] 36. by saving it [1] 37. 6 litres [1]
38. Because flushing with the small button uses less water. [1]
39. a minute [1]
40. By turning the taps off when you are not using them. [1]

Challenge 1

1. breathe in [1]
2. glass bottles [1]
3. ice/hard ice [1]
4. cargo ships [1]

Challenge 2

1. She could not smell as well as he did. [1]
2. To show this is more than just normal listening. [1]
3. On an island near the North Pole: 'he taught her how to listen to the island itself', 'the hard ice of the glaciers in the North Pole'. [3]

Challenge 3

1. At least several weeks, because the narrator says she had been practising for weeks. [2]
2. snowflakes, boats that are too far away to be seen and her dad's sighs [3]
3. No, because Bear is an animal, and animals do not talk. [1]

Challenge 1

1. Aintree [1]
2. a type of boat [1]
3. 1985 [1]
4. stew [1]

Challenge 2

1. The Fab Four [1] 2. Answers may vary, e.g. There will be lots of fascinating things to see. [1]

Challenge 3

1. The text says that Liverpool is perhaps most famous for being their birthplace. [1] 2. Because one protects the sea, and one protects the city. [1] 3. The nickname for people from Liverpool is based on it, and the words 'a city of full bellies' suggests lots of people eat it. [2]

Challenge 1

1. rearrange [1] 2. a) meteorite, b) plane [2] 3. Any two from: glide and wide, alight and night/flight [1]

Challenge 2

1. It is very big. [1] 2. Floating can mean laying still on the surface of water [1], and when birds glide, they do not need to flap their wings [1]. 3. Leaves are light and easily blown about by the wind, so this comparison makes it seem like the bird is also light and easily lifted. [1]

Challenge 3

1. sparkling starfish [2] 2. Answers will vary, e.g. thin, wispy clouds / clouds that you can barely see. [1]
3. The bird seems to enjoy the lights of the city from the way it describes them [1] and it seems proud of the way it lights up the night sky with the planes and meteorites. [1]

Challenge 1

1. Accept any word with a similar meaning to 'gleaming', e.g. shining, bright. **[1] 2.** distort **[1]**
3. Accept any word with a similar meaning to 'emerge', e.g. appear, surface. **[1] 4.** aluminium **[1]**

Challenge 2

1. The rain was falling with great force / it was raining very heavily. **[1] 2.** enormous, colossal **[2] 3. a)** 'shone bright as a penny' **[1] b)** This is effective because the full moon is round and shiny like a metal penny. **[1]**

Challenge 3

1. a giant waking up **[1] 2.** Accept any reasonable answer, e.g. they will be very surprised and may be annoyed or angry that the common has been spoiled, or they may be pleased that they have a nice new supermarket. **[1] 3.** Accept any answer which recognises that the story has a magical element. **[1]**

Challenge 1

1. baby octopus **[1] 2.** foretell **[1] 3.** creature **[1]**
4. Accept any word with a similar meaning to 'tournament', e.g. competition. **[1]**

Challenge 2

1. Accept either mussels or oysters. **[1] 2.** The text describes this as a 'special talent' that Paul has. **[1]**
3. the German flag **[1]**

Challenge 3

1. Because he was given two boxes and had to choose one of them, so he had to pick one team to win. **[1]**
2. Because people want their own team to win. **[1]**
3. Accept any answer supported with reference to the text, e.g. Yes because he got more predictions right than wrong **[1]**.

Challenge 1

1. glossy **[1] 2.** the time in the middle of summer **[1]**
3. darkness **[1]**   4.   snow (also accept icy) **[1]**

Challenge 2

1. Answers will vary, e.g. there are otters playing and otters live in rivers / there is a dragonfly and a kingfisher, and they are found near rivers. **[1]**
2. an emperor dragonfly and a kingfisher **[2]**
3. That it moves quickly. **[1]**

Challenge 3

1. Because it is winter and many trees lose their leaves in winter. **[1]**
2. 'Icy' indicates that the water in the river is cold **[1]** and the word 'held' implies that the fish are hardly moving **[1]**.
3. 'pale shadows' **[1]**

Challenge 1

1. child / children **[1] 2.** Accept any word with a similar meaning to 'twaddle', e.g. rubbish, nonsense. **[1]**
3. revolting **[1]**

Challenge 2

1. Because blisters are unpleasant and unwanted, so this makes the child seem horrible. **[1]**
2. ears **[1]**

Challenge 3

1. a) Parents may think their children are wonderful/ cleverer than they actually are. **[1] b)** Teachers may be more able to see children's faults. **[1]**
2. 'It's the way of the world.' **[1]**
3. The parent may be unhappy or angry **[1]** and they may also be surprised if they thought their child was brilliant **[1]**.

Challenge 1

1. Accept any word with a similar meaning to 'astonishing', e.g. amazing, surprising. **[1]**
2. empty inside **[1]**   3. colour **[1]**

Challenge 2

1. 'Around the world' **[1]**
2. The writer is indicating surprise, as you might not expect an ancient human in France to have seen a rhinoceros and to be able to paint it. **[1]**
3. Any one from: mixing plant sap with ground-up clay to make paint; using leaves or bark to apply the paint; using a reed to blow the paint onto the rock. **[1]**

Challenge 3

1. No because the text says that the cave was 'previously unknown'. **[1]**
2. Because ochre does not decay or fade quickly **[1]** and it lasts longer when not exposed to sunlight and there would have been no sunlight in the cave **[1]**.

Challenge 1

1. Accept any two from: runaway, racing, ever so fast **[2] 2.** clouds / the toy balloon **[1] 3.** a toy balloon **[1]**
4. Female because the narrator refers to it as 'her' – 'chasing her on'. **[1]**

Challenge 2

1. Because the moon shimmers like silver does and is white in colour. **[1] 2.** wind and frost **[2] 3.** Because the stars sparkle like frost. **[1]**

Challenge 3

1. Because the moon appears to be moving fast due to the wind, like a balloon with no string. **[1]**
2. No, because the narrator says, 'But I don't mind' and insists that they saw the moon 'Sailing away'. **[1]**

Answers

3. Accept any reasonable answer that recognises that the narrator is likely to look up to the sky because they are fascinated by how it works **[1]** and because they describe the moon and stars using words that suggest they admire them **[1]**.

Pages 32–35 Progress Test 1

1. The boy keeps tapping, so he really wants to get the spider's attention. **[1]**
2. He blinks a lot. **[1]**
3. He does not want to disturb / scare the spider and just wants to be friendly. **[1]**
4. sincere **[1]**   5. Gives a really big smile. **[1]**
6. To emphasise how badly the spider wants the boy to buy it. **[1]**
7. 'horror or disgust' **[1]**
8. The boy's smile is 'admiring', suggesting he likes how the spider looks. **[1]**
9. Because it didn't want to engage with whoever was tapping on the window. **[1]**
10. It thinks people mustn't be able to see properly. **[1]**
11. He was too different. **[1]**
12. He was expelled. **[1]**   13. develop **[1]**
14. Because they were not like anything they had seen before. **[1]**
15. Ocelots are large animals that can be dangerous. **[1]**
16. famous **[1]**
17. He lived the way he wanted to live. **[1]**
18. Accept any reasonable view, supported by an explanation, e.g. Yes because famous artists do not usually design product logos **[1]**.

Pages 36–38

Challenge 1
1. 12 o'clock / midnight **[1]** 2. Accept any word with a similar meaning to 'sullen', e.g. bad-tempered, sulky. **[1]**
3. announced **[1]** 4. mocked **[1]**

Challenge 2
1. It makes it seem like the silence of the night just went on and on. **[1]** 2. 'Imprisoned' means trapped and 'wakefulness' means being awake **[1]**, so the phrase means Tom could not escape being awake **[1]**.
3. Because the house is quiet **[1]** and he does not want to wake his uncle and aunt **[1]**. 4. He suddenly pays attention. **[1]**

Challenge 3
1. The narrator says Tom's aunt and uncle are always in bed by midnight and usually asleep. **[1]**
2. He compares what the clock does with what 'the clocks would do at home' **[1]**. Also, the fact that he is sleeping in the same house as his aunt and uncle suggests he is visiting them and is not at home **[1]**.

3. People hold their breath when something dramatic is about to happen **[1]**, so when the house seems to do this, it suggests it expects something important is about to happen. **[1]**

Pages 39–41

Challenge 1
1. 'snow-capped' **[1]**
2. Accept any word with a similar meaning to 'footage', e.g. film. **[1]**
3. enthusiasm **[1]**
4. Accept any word with a similar meaning to 'adapting', e.g. changing, improving. **[1]**

Challenge 2
1. Because there are naturally lots of things to play with/on and explore. **[1]**
2. They are both operated by remote control. **[1]**
3. A list of features George wanted his drone to have. **[1]** 4. That his idea quickly became successful and he has sold drones all over the world / that his idea is literally flying high in the sky. **[1]**
5. They are the fastest battery-powered drones in the world. **[1]**

Challenge 3
1. There is no pilot in it so no one will get injured. **[1]**
2. Because they invited him to be a test pilot. **[1]**
3. Because they provide grants to young people and George is young **[1]**, and they thought his idea was a good one **[1]**. 4. Because drones are his passion and he gets to work with them all the time **[1]**, and because he says that work doesn't feel like work when it really interests you **[1]**.

Pages 42–44

Challenge 1
1. stranger **[1]** 2. the kettle **[1]** 3. the clock, the grill **[2]** 4. silence **[1]** 5. glass **[1]**

Challenge 2
1. Answers will vary, e.g. click, clunk. **[1]**
2. Breakfast cereal, for example cornflakes **[1]** because the whole verse is about breakfast **[1]**.
3. Toast **[1]**, because the text has referred to the 'popping of the toaster' **[1]** and the knife makes a 'scraping sound' which is the sound you get when you spread something on toast **[1]**.
4. Because frying food makes a hissing sound. **[1]**
5. 'bubbling of the bathtub' **[1]**

Challenge 3
1. The stranger puts the sounds in a bag **[1]** which is odd because sounds are not things you can pick up and move **[1]**.
2. Sad **[1]**, because a lot of the sounds mentioned are pleasant sounds, and the narrator says 'Life will never be the same again' **[1]**.

3. Accept any reasonable answer supported by a reason. **[1]**

Challenge 1

1. A song sung by one person. **[1] 2.** competitor **[1]**
3. 'Clouding' suggests the frown darkens her face and makes it look angry, like a cloud covering the sun. **[1]**
4. math **[1]**

Challenge 2

1. Soojin's pencil **[1]** because later in the text, Amina feels the pencil in her side 'again' showing that it was the pencil the first time too **[1]**.
2. Julie likes to be the centre of attention. **[1]**
3. singing loudly **[1]**
4. That she finds it difficult to get her words out clearly. **[1]**
5. Because they are in class and the teacher does not want them to talk to each other. **[1]**

Challenge 3

1. Because she thinks about singing in front of a crowd and this make her feel nervous **[1]** and feeling nervous can make your stomach feel like it is tied in knots **[1]**.
2. She would be nervous in front of the judges **[1]** so her throat would go dry and her voice would sound croaky, if she could even sing at all **[1]**.
3. Amina can sing well and Julie can't **[1]**. Amina is shy and Julie likes to be the centre of attention **[1]**.
4. Accept any reasonable answer, e.g. Yes, because Soojin will convince her she sings very well. **[1]**

Challenge 1

1. drawing pictures **[1] 2.** Accept any word with a similar meaning to 'narrative', e.g. story. **[1] 3.** Accept any word with a similar meaning to 'images', e.g. pictures. **[1] 4.** college **[1] 5.** heard by accident

Challenge 2

1. her childhood memories **[1]   2.** the pictures **[1]**
3. She says she was 'unprepared for the work it takes to produce a finished book'. **[1]**
4. She wrote and drew at the same time. **[1]**

Challenge 3

1. Child was surprised her first book interested a publisher because she was very young **[1]** and was later rejected 'over and over again' by publishers, showing how hard it is to get a book published **[1]**.
2. She worked out what it was she wanted to say **[1]**; we know it worked because her books were published in the end **[1]**.
3. It was difficult at the time **[1]**, but now she thinks it taught her to be determined **[1]**.

4. She tells us the Clarice Bean stories are based on her childhood memories **[1]** and that some of the things she remembers are 'funny and peculiar' **[1]**.

Challenge 1

1. sag **[1] 2.** Accept any word with a similar meaning to 'corridors', e.g. hallways, passages. **[1] 3.** Accept any word with a similar meaning to 'beasts', e.g. animals, creatures. **[1] 4.** a short or light sleep **[1] 5.** Accept any word with a similar meaning to 'glow', e.g. gleam. **[1]**

Challenge 2

1. having no energy **[1]**
2. neon lights and video screens **[2]**
3. By telling them what to do, or not to do. **[1]**
4. Because they 'ignore' our way of life. **[1]**
5. 'Through the Cat on your lap' **[1]**

Challenge 3

1. A battery stores energy **[1]** so the poet is saying that the cat stores energy that flows into its owner **[1]**.
2. You stroke the cat **[1]** and the power will 'flow' into your hands **[1]**. **3.** To remind us that domestic cats are related to big cats **[1]** and that they are therefore very powerful **[1]**.

1. Finds out about the stars and space. **[1]**
2. Accept any two from: library books, own books, star globe. **[1]**
3. Stars or space **[1]**, because the narrator is very interested in this and has lots of other space-related things **[1]**.
4. So they would glow at night and look like the night sky inside the bedroom. **[1]**
5. begged **[1]**   6.   sphere **[1]**
7. Because the narrator says it showed 'a different constellation every time you switched it on'. **[1]**
8. you completely memorise it **[1]**
9. Because even though it contains lots of constellations, the narrator has memorised them all which shows they have looked at it often. **[2]**
10. Draws or creates pictures for books. **[1]**
11. No, because the text says most people thought insects were 'disgusting'. **[1]**
12. That they turn into butterflies. **[1]**
13. drastically **[1]**   14.   two **[1]**
15. South America **[1]**
16. If you 'brave something' it means you have to show courage in order to do it, which suggests that Maria's visit to the rainforest was difficult or dangerous. **[1]**
17. 1679 and 1705 **[1]**
18. 'became a hit all over Europe' **[1]**
19. the detail **[1]**

Pages 58–61

Challenge 1

1. it is white [1] 2. early morning / sunrise / daybreak [1] 3. Accept any word with a similar meaning to 'clambered', e.g. climbed or scrambled. [1] 4. striding [1]

Challenge 2

1. That he is asleep. [1] 2. To scare the lion off if it won't go away. [1] 3. It made a groaning sound like a yawn [1] and was wide open, like a yawning mouth [1]. 4. Because lions hunt elephants for food. [1] 5. Put in prison or in a cage. [1]

Challenge 3

1. Because it is not light yet, what looked like a clump of trees in the gloom [1] turned out to be a herd of elephants when it was closer to the narrator and he could see it clearly [1]. 2. It had been tame / living in captivity. [1] 3. No, because he has shown the lion affection so far [1]; he is only pretending to hate it so it will not follow him home, because he wants it to be free [1]. 4. Because he loves the lion and so he is upset about frightening it away [1], and he knows he will miss it if it does run away [1]. 5. Accept any reasonable answer based on the information in the text, e.g. Bertie might get into trouble for setting the lion free. [1]

Pages 62–65

Challenge 1

1. Accept any word with a similar meaning to 'fascinating', e.g. interesting, captivating. [1] 2. Accept any word with a similar meaning to 'wonders', e.g. amazing things. [1] 3. prosper [1] 4. beat [1] 5. They were scratched on the floor of the desert/drawn into the landscape. [1]

Challenge 2

1. 'Potatoes' and 'Piggies' [1] 2. Because there are lots of amazing things to see there. [1] 3. a) Cotahuasi Canyon, b) any one from Nazca Lines, Puente de Piedra or Machu Picchu [2] 4. Yes, because the stones are stuck together with eggs. [1] 5. Accept any two from: they grew potatoes, they used the potato as a measure of time, they built the city of Machu Picchu. [2]

Challenge 3

1. They are 'uncontacted' / live separately from the modern world [1]. 2. They were used to stick bricks together for the Puente de Piedra [1] and the bridge is still standing after 400 years [1]. 3. Because nobody knows why they were created or how [1]. 4. It could suggest it is high up [1] or on the edge of something, like a bird perched in a tree [1].

Pages 66–69

Challenge 1

1. companion [1]

2. Accept any word with a similar meaning to 'blossoms', e.g. flowers, blooms. [1]

3. the hillside [1]   4. fuzz [1]

Challenge 2

1. You hear it blowing. [1] 2. rain and wind [1] 3. play as much as you want [1] 4. flying [1] 5. A child [1], because he describes himself as a 'little boy' [1].

Challenge 3

1. the eyes [1] 2. The arrival of spring will make him feel happier because sunshine is associated with happiness. [1] 3. They are both small and sweet. [1] 4. The narrator does not like winter [1] because he wants spring to 'sweep away' the snow and sleet / he is clearly very happy about the arrival of spring [1]. 5. There might be fewer signs of nature changing (e.g. trees and wildflowers). [1]

Pages 70–73

Challenge 1

1. A regulation that says that people must stay inside between specified hours. [1]

2. Accept any word with a similar meaning to 'mighty', e.g. powerful, huge. [1]

3. wilted [1]

4. everlasting [1]

Challenge 2

1. 50 years [1] 2. To draw attention to the ways people harmed the Earth [1] and how many different ways they did it [1] 3. 'Lights had to be out at eight o'clock sharp.' [1] 4. The ash of burned trees and volcanoes. [2] 5. Because the words 'perfect' and 'gold' make it seem precious. [1]

Challenge 3

1. The ash in the air from the volcanoes blocked the sunlight from reaching the Earth. [1]

2. Stars [1], because Alfred is imagining what the night sky would have looked like before the moon and stars became invisible [1].

3. Snow is white [1] and when a person is ill their skin often looks much paler than normal, so if Alfred is white like snow, he must be very ill [1].

4. The text says 'Thank goodness' he had books, suggesting he likes them [1]. It also says history books are his 'absolute favourite', suggesting he has read and enjoyed different types of books [1].

5. You need light to read by [1], and as part of the curfew, lights had to be out by 8 o'clock [1].

Pages 74–77

Challenge 1

1. Accept any word with a similar meaning to 'motion', e.g. movement. [1]

2. Accept any word with a similar meaning to 'ripples', e.g. waves. [1]